" Perfect timing for property advice

The timing of this very valuable book couldn't have been better, or of more use. The public at large are getting many, many messages in regard to the current property market and the doomsayers keep adding to the pessimism.

These highly qualified authors have put together a very interesting and I think valuable suite of thinking that anyone can benefit from, given the present state of play in the property market.

I'd especially recommend this to the real estate industry and those in search of enlightened, thoughtful advice based on expertise and experience. — *Hawkes Bay Today* "

" Gloomy outlook need not be end

Investors should be focusing on making sure they have strong enough foundations to survive a falling property market, reckons author Peter Aranyi.

How To Survive and Prosper in a Falling Property Market ... doesn't try to predict a collapse of property prices, but concludes there are some pretty staunch indicators which should warn investors to take care for tough times ahead.

That message is needed because there are still plenty of spruikers continuing to predict high returns on property despite today's sky-high prices.

Aranyi said the book was in part designed as 'an antidote' to what he calls 'the foolhardy and frankly deceptive sales spiel of property spruikers of all shades.' Investors need to shock-proof their property portfolios. — *Sunday Star Times* "

About the authors — investors teaching investors

Andrew King is the author of two best-selling books, *Create Wealth: The Complete Guide to Residential Property Investment* and *Planning for Property Success*. As a long-time officeholder in various property investor associations, Andrew is a high-profile and respected media spokesman on residential property.

Mike McCombie has 25 years of hands-on experience as a residential and commercial property investor. Mike has been involved in virtually every facet of commercial property investment and development. He has taught principles of successful investment at training courses on both sides of the Tasman and recorded a popular DVD video programme *Proven Formulas for Success in Commercial Real Estate*.

Mark Withers is a specialist property accountant, advisor, residential and commercial investor and the author of *Property Tax*. Mark's practical and plain-talking advice is based on years of experience dealing with thousands of transactions for his clients and his own investment property portfolio.

Tony Steindle is a lawyer whose practice covers all aspects of real estate law. His clients include investors of all sorts, as well as developers and commercial landlords. Tony is the author of *Property Law* and a sought-after advisor and speaker on legal issues affecting property investors.

Peter Aranyi is the author of *Commercial Real Estate Investor's Guide* and editor of several best-selling books on property investment. His training company Empower Education is a trusted source of practical and impartial information — and part of the success of thousands of property investors throughout Australasia.

Read more from these authors at **www.EmpowerEducation.com**

How to Survive and Prosper in a Falling Property Market

... and other vital secrets to building wealth through real estate

Edited by Peter Aranyi

EMPOWER LEADERS PUBLISHING

To Pearl, Amelia and Kit — the A team

First published 2008, revised and reprinted 2008 (twice)
Compiled and edited by Peter Aranyi
Book design and production by Peter Aranyi
Cover design by Jon Evans, Critical Mass Communications
Printed by Publishing Press

National Library of New Zealand Cataloguing-in-Publication Data

How to survive and prosper in a falling property market : and
other vital secrets to building wealth through real estate / edited
by Peter Aranyi. 1st ed.
Includes index.
ISBN 978-0-9582307-5-9
1. Real estate investment—New Zealand. 2. Real estate
business—New Zealand. 3. Finance, Personal—New Zealand.
4. Recessions—New Zealand. I. Aranyi, Peter, 1958-
332.63240993—dc 22

EMPOWER
LEADERS™
Empower Leaders Publishing Ltd
PO Box 38 226 Howick, Auckland 2145, New Zealand
in association with Empower Education Ltd
+64 9 535 2415 • www.EmpowerLeaders.co.nz

Contents

Mike McCombie

Mark Withers

13. Survive and prosper in times of financial adversity

Tony Steindle

14. Navigating the legal issues when times get tough

Why this book?

The purpose of this book is to share experience with you in the hope that you can learn from lessons others have learned the hard way. This is not a book of 'predictions', nor does it warn of an impending crash or meltdown … except to point out that there is a pattern in the property cycle. This pattern repeats. It's not exactly the same every time, but significant changes occur in the market and they tend to do so in a form that resembles previous changes.

It's worth being aware of the pattern and knowing how resulting pressures affect various players in the market. In the past people have been financially burned as a result of their ignorance of the changing cycle and its flow-on effects.

Unfortunately, there's no fun way to pass on some of the negative things that can and do happen to property owners, investors and businesses. Nor is there any point glossing over the turmoil that occurs from time to time in the property and financial markets. People suffer from these changes. Our aim in this book is take a good hard look at the downside as well as the upside — and to identify ways you can firstly protect yourself and secondly be in a position to make the most of the opportunities that inevitably arise.

It doesn't matter whether you think the market is hot, cold or indifferent as you read this. We've done our best to produce a useful handbook with principles that apply *throughout* the cycle. This is not your 'complete guide to success' in property, nor do we say it's the only book you should read (see recommended reading). In part, we've also worked to offer an antidote to some of the foolhardy and frankly deceptive sales spiel of property spruikers of all shades. There's an old saying: 'Never ask an encyclopaedia salesman if it's a good time to buy an encyclopaedia.' The answer will always be 'yes'. Too many investors and home buyers seek advice solely from those who would benefit directly from the transaction. People who act in this way are the traditional losers or victims of the property cycle. Do not copy them.

Get professional legal, financial and tax advice on your own situation and any proposed course of action. A useful strategy for success is to seek a range of sources of neutral, impartial information from people with *relevant* experience.

This book is a start.

Stay up to date — register for your free newsletter at www.EmpowerEducation.com

For the *latest information* on this and other important property investment-related subjects, visit www.EmpowerEducation.com and join the mailing list.

1

Introduction

Moving forward as an investor by regarding the past

cycle *noun*
[often with adj.] a series of events that are regularly repeated in the same order: *the boom and slump periods of a trade cycle.*

— Concise Oxford Dictionary

'The property cycle' is the name we give to a model which describes the variations in the state of the real estate market. At its purest, the cycle rotates through boom, slump, bust, recovery. These stages can be reported as a 'strong', 'firm' or 'hot' market on the upswing and a 'weak', 'soft' or 'cooling' market on the downswing.

Fundamentally, the property cycle is concerned with supply and demand. When there are more buyers than there are properties for sale ('a seller's market'), prices and values rise. When buyers are scarce and the amount of stock for sale grows to the level of oversupply ('a buyer's market'), prices remain static or fall.

In a boom, desperate buyers can pay too much — and in a slump, desperate sellers sell too cheaply. Most buyers don't have to buy and most sellers don't have to sell. They can ride this part of the cycle out. The pressure comes on when someone is in a forced situation — e.g. an owner needs to sell to take up a job transfer or an investor must reduce debt.

Trend lines

When considering a market and its variations, one of the most useful things you can look at is a trend line — often drawn as an average through a set of points on a graph (see example below).

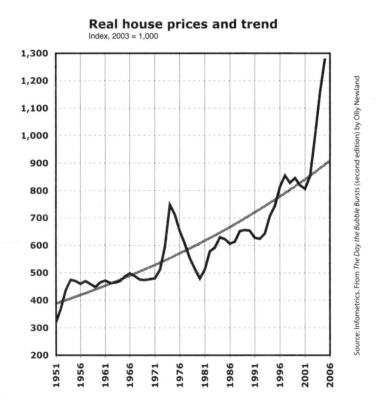

Real house prices and trend
Index, 2003 = 1,000

Source: Infometrics. From *The Day the Bubble Bursts* (second edition) by Olly Newland

Figure 1.1   Example of price data and trend line

Statisticians and economists favour trend lines because they imply a general course or demonstrate a tendency, in some cases even pointing to a vaguely stable equilibrium.

In the case of real estate, for instance, economists might say that over time, property prices rise at 'about the rate of general inflation'. Alternatively, they might try to reference this price growth to GDP (Gross Domestic Product) growth … or to net population growth … or any other index or 'X factor' they've identified. Market values, prices, volumes, interest rates, etc, can all be analysed and plotted, then identified as presently above or below the trend line. The expectation is that any outstanding rise above the trend line (or fall below it) will be *temporary* and that the values will revert to the trend line — usually through a 'correction' in the appropriate direction.

History and experience tells us that a period of exceptional price growth or high level of activity in a market is usually followed by an adjustment — a drop-off in price growth and activity, and sometimes by a time of stagnant or negative growth. The high is followed by a low. A hot market cools. The boom turns into a slump.

A general rule is that the larger the rise, the sharper the fall that follows. This is not true in all cases. Yes, the property market changes, but not every cyclic fluctuation is characterised by a raging boom followed by a crash. Just as some parties are more fun than others, market variations differ in nature and intensity. Markets can crash, or they can soften gradually or stagnate. They can also undergo a long gentle rise — not every upswing of the cycle leads to a boom. As we'll see, the energy that sometimes turns a boom into an over-heated bubble is a mass over-confidence. Sometimes called market hysteria, this super-positive view of a commodity actually becomes both a cause and an effect.

When property (or a property sector) becomes a fad or flavour of the month, when everyone is doing it or enthusiastically talking about it in the same way as sharemarket mania, that's when the property market will, sooner or later, be in line for a correction.

Not just 'one' cycle

The property cycle is always turning. The market isn't the same for long. It's also splintered and fragmented. The market in a region, even a town, can be independently going through its own cycle — rising or falling due to factors affecting local supply and demand. Further, segments of a market (e.g. apartments, rental areas, commercial, industrial, retail, office) can have their own cycle and rhythm.

Certain types of investments can become fashionable — remember supply and demand — sometimes for reasons which are quite out of the ordinary. For instance, the childcare industry and eldercare industry have both in recent years been the target of efforts to consolidate ownership. For a time, larger overseas companies had their chequebooks out trying to buy up any reasonable childcare centre or retirement village on the market. This buying activity tended to create a seller's market and prices increased. Any local buyers had to outbid the offshore buyers. The same temporary effect happened in the funeral home business, and some years earlier in the office products/retail stationery business as national chains were created by amalgamating small independent operations. Staying close to your market and knowing what's happening in it is your best defence against mistakes and can alert you to opportunities.

However, the increased speed of communication (the global village) and the funds circulating the planet looking for higher yields mean that in the larger picture, individual markets are less isolated ... and more interconnected. A decision by the US Federal Reserve to raise or lower interest rates can quickly affect the financial markets in Australia and

New Zealand. A decision made by a bank board in Geneva, London or Sydney (influenced at least in part by local market conditions, or global sentiment and events) can flow through to lending policies throughout Australia and New Zealand — depressing a small local or regional market because of factors that, on the surface, have nothing whatsoever to do with local conditions.

A correction, when it comes, can be national, regional or local. There's often a time lag as effects roll out, and some areas can remain stagnant — like rock pools: still full of water although the tide has gone out.

The cycle is neutral — neither 'good' nor 'bad'

Despite the pejorative language some people use to describe the market at any time (strong/weak, positive/negative, good/bad, hot/cold, active/slow, etc) the market is no more good or bad than any natural cycle. Like the weather or the tides, there's no part of this cycle that is wrong. It just is.

As you'll read, Mike McCombie's suggestion to consider your digestive cycle is highly relevant: which segment of this quintessentially natural cycle should you try to avoid? Eating? Digesting? Excreting? The answer is, none of the above. Each part of the digestive cycle is crucial.

As an investor, it's your job to tailor your decision-making and actions to be *appropriate* to the market — for instance, as Mike says, don't buy vacant commercial buildings at the bottom of the cycle unless you have a fairly solid plan for turning that situation around. Trying to lease vacant commercial space in a flat or depressed economy can be a recipe for struggle. (However, if you have a prospective tenant, or a plan to, for example, change the property's use to something that is in demand, then the investment has possibilities). Or, as Andrew King points out, there comes a time when it's more useful for a residential investor to target 'do-up' properties where value can be fairly easily added, rather than struggling to find a rental property that meets your investment criteria.

Interestingly, often the 'right' or useful action to take will be the exact opposite of what the majority does — a counter-cyclical approach. As Warren Buffett says, "We simply attempt to be fearful when others are greedy, and to be greedy only when others are fearful."
Likewise, don't waste time trying to make banks and lenders 'wrong' or 'bad' for protecting their self-interests by changing their rules. Lenders are, first and foremost, in the business of staying in business. Protect your own interests — particularly from them!

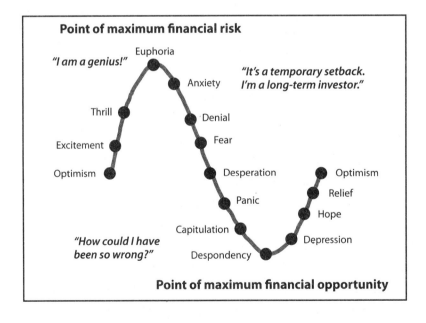

Figure 1.2   The cycle of market emotions
Most often quoted by advisors in the sharemarket, this classic representation of the stages of market confidence can also apply to real estate. When confidence plummets, experienced investors start looking for bargains.

The real driver: market confidence or 'social mood'

As we stated in *Commercial Real Estate Investor's Guide*, the property market is driven by **emotion** and **sentiment**. Many of the so-called 'drivers' quoted (really market indicators in our view) like household head count and number of listings are just reflections of the real driver: market confidence. Identify the level of market confidence at any given time and you'll be close to the market.

Some market observers label this phenomenon 'social mood' and note that it reflects the human tendency for herding behaviour. Social mood can change, quickly, and with it the idea of what a smart investment is in a given market. When market confidence is high (i.e. the social mood is positive and optimistic) people, companies and institutions take on risks or debt they may not really be able to afford. Their optimism leads them to enter into transactions with very poor fundamentals — or blinds them to the riskiness of their position. When the social mood turns from positive to negative, fear replaces greed, and people begin to see these risky behaviours or positions more accurately.

In a rapidly rising housing market the belief that property prices 'can only increase' is all-pervasive. A stall in price growth, or a reversal, or a series of negative market events like company collapses, can change that belief (and sometimes it's stubbornly-held) before being widely acknowledged.

Experienced investors have seen these market corrections before. They know they are just part of how things work. In his book *The Bubble of American Supremacy*, financier George Soros explains how a market 'bubble' comes about:

> The process begins when a *prevailing trend* and a *prevailing bias* reinforce each other. As the bias becomes more pronounced, it becomes vulnerable to being corrected by the evidence. As long as the trend survives the test, it serves

to reinforce the bias so that the bias can become quite far removed from reality. Eventually, there arrives a moment of truth, when participants become aware of *the gap that separates their views from reality.* A twilight period, when the trend is no longer reinforced by the belief, ensues. In due course the trend is also reversed and *a self-correcting process is set in motion in the opposite direction.* Depending on how far a boom-bust process has carried, the reversal can be quite catastrophic, similar to a bubble's bursting. [emphasis added]

Adopting Soros's language, in a hot real estate market the prevailing trend = 'property prices rising', and the prevailing bias = 'property prices can only rise'.

These two factors can combine to create a period of market exuberance, in some cases over-exuberance, which must ultimately correct. That's the market cycle in action. What's unfortunate is that it is often the new players or late entrants to the market who pay the price in a downwards correction. As veteran commercial real estate agent Tim Julian says:

To some extent the length of a short cycle is determined by *the period it takes to forget the pain of the last adjustment from market over-exuberance.* This is achieved in the overall market by new decision-makers emerging who either were not around during the last cycle or were so junior or simple that the events made little impact on them. [emphasis added]

On the late entrants being the biggest losers, Warren Buffett puts it this way:

It's like most trends: At the beginning, it's driven by fundamentals, then speculation takes over. As the old saying goes, what the wise man does in the beginning, fools do in the end. With any asset class that has a big move, first the fundamentals attract speculation, then the speculation becomes dominant. Once a price history develops, and people hear that their neighbour made a lot of money on something, that impulse takes over. ... Orgies tend to be wildest toward the end. It's like being Cinderella at the ball. You know that at midnight everything's going to turn back to pumpkins and mice. But you look around and say, 'one more dance,' and so does everyone else. The party does get to be more fun — and besides, there are no clocks on the wall. And then suddenly the clock strikes 12, and everything turns back to pumpkins and mice. [CNN *Money* magazine May 2006]

Being merely a summation of human decisions, markets are almost by definition uncertain. As Buffett said, there are no clocks on the wall. There's no timer on the scoreboard counting down the time remaining before the sports teams are to change ends. To keep themselves safe, investors must exercise vigilance. Watch the market. ***Watch its mood.***

By all means, look at the statistics and the economic analysis. They do tell a story too, but, as we've discussed, they're generally not very predictive. It's not the statistics themselves, but rather the market's reaction to them, which is important. Sometimes markets can shrug off bad news, at other times confidence can slump, even crash.

Beware pseudo-science

Be wary of pseudo-academic discussion and analysis around 'drivers' and 'influencers' of the property cycle. Some amateur economists and self-proclaimed property investment experts are, sadly, 'gums for hire' — and their services are used as bait by property promoters.

On the other hand, many genuinely qualified, professional economists are fine people, but, with respect, *they* sometimes appear to forget economics is a social science (not one of the 'hard' sciences like physics). They also seem fond of over-complicating things, being dutifully rigorous with statistics and mathematics when the numbers they're working with remain fairly nebulous.

No amount of bamboozle factor with statistics ("Oh, look, business confidence has fallen 2.6% this month!") can make up for the hazy nature of this type of 'data'. Let's make a distinction between *hard historical data* and the 'opinion', 'intentions' or 'confidence' measures favoured by the media.

Sometimes the sample size for such so-called statistics is so small (or self-referencing) it makes variations irrelevant. At others the opinion questionnaire basis for the data ('Is this a good time to buy?' or 'Do you expect business will be better next year?') is woolly or indistinct. While there is value in examining a *trend* in this sort of data, it's dubious to regard individual samples, swings or data points as trustworthy, despite their ready acceptance by a hungry news media.

On factors such as exchange rate variations, income levels, household or business sector debt, consumer spending, export figures and interest rates (hard historical data), economists and analysts can be a *great* source of information and interpretation. And this type of data can be very illuminating, sometimes even useful, to you as an investor.

Some of the brains looking at the market are the best in the business and can identify what's been going on (hindsight) in terms of investment fundamentals, taking into account inflation, mortgage interest rates, rents received and tax rates. From experience, however, many of their 'predictions' can turn on a dime — the analysts change their forecasts with great alacrity. And you can't blame them for this. "When the facts change, I change my mind. What do you do, sir?" economist John Maynard Keynes once famously responded to a charge of inconsistency.

In many cases, such commentary is little more than hindsight — some of it practised by self-appointed experts. A wise investor sees this as 'noise' and looks for real-world, specific data *for their specific market* — 'hard' factors such as up-to-date comparative sales prices and rents/leases being received.

Another trap for amateur economists is mixing up causes and effects. For example, the average number of days to sell a property varies depending on the strength of the market, which it *reflects*. It seems faintly absurd to describe this measure as a *driver* of the market. Similarly, rental levels can be seen as an indicator of market supply and demand not a driver of it. (Of course, investors will make decisions based on rental levels and factor in their effect on return on investment — but these are the tail, not the dog.)

There's value in considering these factors, their trends, and being aware of market commentary, but it's *not* just arithmetic. Market sentiment and confidence — optimism and pessimism — are the indicators we observe most closely.

It is difficult to improve on Olly Newland's evaluation from *The Day the Bubble Bursts*:

> It would be easy to spend several lifetimes 'analysing', in a rigorous statistical fashion, the factors that drive the Economic or Property Clock. Pointy-heads can and do bury themselves in statistics, rows of data, multicoloured charts and graphs, finally emerging triumphant at having weighed all the macro-economic factors (interest rates, money supply, immigration, etc) and coming up with a theory to 'explain' what happens as the cycle moves around the clock. (But always after the fact. With very few exceptions, their self-serving 'predictions' aren't worth a tinker's cuss.)
>
> But the real driver is emotion or 'market sentiment'. What emerges in markets is a scaled-up version of 'group think', where the pervasive mood switches (and I mean switches) from negative to positive, then gradually becomes super-positive and hyped-up. In other words, hysterical.
>
> Unfortunately, the reversal of sentiment happens a lot more suddenly. There's an old saying from the sharemarket: 'The bull climbs up the stairs, but the bear jumps out the window.' (And I've lived it.) The climb towards high market mania happens regularly.

The cycle is not *completely* predictable
— nor is it signposted

There's another old stockmarket saying, 'No-one rings a bell at the top or bottom of the market'.

Hearing about the property cycle, its repetitive pattern, the drivers and indicators that routinely sweep through the market and economy, and its overall rhythm, less-experienced investors can imagine that the cycle operates like a set of traffic lights — perfectly synchronised, orderly and with clear indications for all sides to see. Actually, this is not the case. It's the very lack of precise predictability and clarity that causes many of the casualties (and opportunities).

The phases of the property cycle are not signposted like rural towns. You won't see a banner that states 'Welcome to the slump' or 'You are now entering a commercial rent downturn' or 'Farewell from stagnant house price growth. Invest safely. Come back soon.' If only it were that simple.

In fact the market is beset with false starts and lulls, in the same way a faulty automatic gearbox sometimes 'hunts' for the right gear to engage when the car is driven uphill. As you'll see later in this book, inexperience, bad advice, and fear (fear of missing out and, later, fear of loss) can lead people to make unfavourable buying, selling and investing decisions. Some investors can sound like impatient children (*Are we there yet? Are we there yet?*).

Things are always so much clearer in hindsight. Take some advice from Olly Newland who advocates patience:

> Real estate is all about timing.
> Write it on your forehead and never forget it.

The purpose of this book is not to scare or to depress you. Rather, we've aimed to share the experience of those who have been through the cycle to help you stay safe and prosper. Use this first to raise your awareness. Then by taking some of the steps outlined here, you can build your financial strength to withstand the pressures and make the most of opportunities that present themselves.

As you read, look out for themes. Often when introducing one of our seminars or training courses, I stress that we don't shrink from repetition; in fact we welcome it.

If you read the same piece of advice (or different facets of it) from several of the contributors to this book, that's a *good* thing. The emphasis means it's important! If you read investor Mike McCombie's warning about a trap based on his hard experience, then see it reinforced by lawyer Tony Steindle who's seen that particular trap hurt a few of his clients, perhaps you will get the message that they're trying to share a *vital* piece of advice. A point like 'Always get your agreements in writing' is stressed repeatedly, so take the hint. It may be of use to you. We hope so, and wish you well.

— Peter Aranyi, *editor.*

Share your feedback and success stories

We'd love to have your feedback and hear about your adventures applying what you've learnt from this book.
Please write to:

Success Stories
c/- Empower Leaders Publishing
PO Box 38 226, Howick, Auckland 2145,
New Zealand

or email with 'Success Stories' as the subject line to:
info@EmpowerLeaders.co.nz

2

Residential property investment in a downturn

Andrew King

Property investment has been and still is a great way for Kiwis and Australians to create wealth and provide an income for their retirement. During boom times many people believe that property investment is a one-way bet (i.e. 'you can't lose').

Times change however, and when they do it isn't quite so easy to make an investment in property work as well. In fact, as the market cools, more and more people start to realise that property *isn't* a one-way investment after all and that a downturn could hit them hard.

Different investors will face different situations, but every investor needs to consider that as the market changes, their investment strategies should also change.

How the market changes with the cycle

A bit of recent history

Looking back to 2002, house prices started their upward trend apparently fuelled by high levels of immigration. In my view, the seeds for that price growth had been planted long before. Average rental yields for New Zealand were around 10%, house prices had been static since 1998; the country's economy was performing well; incomes had risen over the previous four years; and the average two-year fixed interest rate was 7.5%.

At the beginning of this boom, it was relatively easy for investors to buy a rental property where the rent covered the outgoings — a 'cash flow positive' investment. Cash flow aside, faced with the likelihood of increasing house prices, many ordinary properties made good investments, especially when considering the potential for capital gains.

The boom ran its course — with the strongest and most sustained rise in house prices since the 1970s. The popularity of property investment ballooned. Books on the subject (including two of mine) flew off the shelves and up the best seller lists, property seminars proliferated and new businesses sprang up to feed the demand for rental property investments.

As always, sentiment began to change towards the top of the market. Five years after the NZ boom started, the market looked very different. The immigration boom dwindled, average residential rental yields had dropped by 35% and mortgage interest rates were significantly higher. A 'credit crunch' and house price slump in the US affected investor confidence around the world. Several local finance companies — the source of much property development funding — collapsed.

Changes in the market

Throughout the property cycle different investors are affected in different ways.

At the top of a market, and in the early stages of a downturn, would-be investors find it difficult to make the numbers work so they can actually enter the market as investors. Bullish new investors who enthusiastically bought large amounts of investment property during the 'up' cycle find that while they have increased their equity, they struggle with cash flow. This is especially pronounced when their fixed interest rate terms come to an end. Long term investors (with lower borrowings) may not have the same cash flow problems; however they may still be unable to finance the lifestyle they want.

A key piece of advice can be taken from Douglas Adams's wonderful *The Hitch-hikers Guide to the Galaxy*:

DON'T PANIC

When property cycles change there are always good and bad outcomes. Among those seen as bad when the market slumps are:

1) In the short term, the market will no longer effortlessly make you wealthy or cover your mistakes by increasing the value of your property.

2) It will be harder for you to purchase new rental property without suffering a significant deficit in cash flow.

3) Your existing property may become difficult to fund as a result of interest rate increases.

The good news, however, is that there'll be reduced competition from other investors and first home buyers, plus a higher proportion of people who *have* to sell — leading to good buying opportunities.

As an investor, there are different strategies you can use to make the most of changing situations. If you can successfully purchase a property — and hold onto it —in these market conditions, things will probably only get better a few years later.

In a downturn some, perhaps many, investors will believe that they *have* to sell due to the changing market conditions. In fact they may not need to, but if they don't take steps to address changing circumstances they could find themselves in a position where they are *forced* to sell. Avoid this at all costs. Your key aim should be to keep control of the situation. You need to develop a strong and detailed plan of action for the present and the future.

Like most good plans, this will involve taking stock of what is happening in the market and what you see as likely to happen in the future. You need to forecast how you could be affected, how you would *prefer* to be affected — and what you can proactively do to work things in your favour.

It is useful to have an idea of how the property cycle works so you can see why you need to change your investment strategies at different times. Remember that changing market conditions affect different investors differently. It's impossible for one strategy to be right for all investors, all the time. Depending on their financial position, some investors will need to focus on *survival*—others may actually benefit from the downturn.

The property cycle

At its most basic interpretation, the property cycle reflects supply and demand. If the supply of properties is insufficient to meet demand then prices are likely to rise. If the supply of properties is excessive to demand, then prices tend to fall. It is, of course, more complicated than this —mostly due to human behaviour.

In a perfect world, business and investing decisions would not be affected by emotions. But consider events such as the dot-com boom where investors got caught up in the excitement and let emotions such as greed, fear, envy and impatience get in the way of good business decision making.

The housing market is affected to a large degree by emotional considerations, as around 70% of house sale and purchase transactions are for homes rather than investment properties. The investor looking to buy a rental property operates in the same market as first home buyers and people upgrading their home — both classes of buyer who tend to be emotional — as well as other investors. This emotional factor complicates the housing market.

The boom phase

The boom phase of the property cycle can start off quite slowly, but once it picks up pace it takes time to slow down again. Generally, a boom is sparked by an increase in demand which outstrips existing supply and isn't met by an adequate increase in supply. Sometimes it's sparked by increases in the cost of building new homes which pulls up the value of existing homes.

Factors that affect changes in the supply of residential property generally occur slowly. Supply is affected by such factors as local government regulations and district plans, economic conditions, and the length of time it takes developers to sense a demand, then create a new subdivision and actually construct houses within it.

Some key factors affecting demand for residential property are immigration levels, natural population growth and the number of people per household. The most volatile factors are immigration and the number of people per household.

When these two factors change they can affect the value of property quickly. This is because immigrants usually require somewhere to live straight away so if immigration is up, there is an instant increase in demand for residential dwellings. Natural population growth (i.e. more births than deaths) is often accommodated within existing homes, so it doesn't have such an immediate effect on demand.

This time lag between an increase in demand for property and the increase in supply increases competition for available property and hence prices rise.

As the market progresses through its growth phase, property prices increase while rental prices and incomes tend not to keep pace. The Reserve Bank increases interest rates in an attempt to dampen down the inflationary effects of higher property prices while attempting to talk the market down with warnings about what it considered 'excessive' borrowing and spending. Property becomes less affordable as prices and interest rates rise.

As the boom phase continues, property becomes even *less* affordable and demand tends to fall away. Would-be first home buyers who were either unable or unwilling to purchase in the early stages of the property cycle growth period start to feel the pinch. With increasing house prices and interest rates, they become disillusioned with the quality of property they can afford.

As house price growth outstrips rental price growth, aspiring first home buyers see current rents as a bargain (it's cheaper to rent than buy) and put off their purchase decisions — increasing the demand for rental accommodation. It can take landlords a little while to notice this change in the market, as many are amateurs (literally hobbyists) so rental prices do not immediately increase.

The fundamentals for property investors slide further out of kilter (e.g. rental yields drop) and it becomes more and more difficult for an investor to purchase ordinary property and obtain the same rental return.

Many investors drop out because they find it difficult to make the figures work. Rental yields tend to be lower and interest costs higher — making it harder for investors to purchase new rental property.

As a consequence of first home buyers and part-time investors withdrawing from the market, the *volume of property sales* starts to fall and the *number of days* it takes to sell a property starts to increase. *Prices* may actually continue to rise, however, due to a phenomenon where sellers take their property off the market if they can't get what they want—temporarily reducing supply. They sometimes put them back on the market again some months later in a second attempt to get their asking price.

Additionally, some enthusiastic buyers can also keep property prices growing. These late starters sometimes feel they have to buy something or they will 'miss' the property wave. They believe the claims of property marketers, developers and property finders that everything is still positive for future price rises. These investors are attracted by advertisements claiming that you can buy an apartment for "just $1,000 deposit" and "let the tenant and taxman pay off the mortgage" (that should be on a Tui billboard. "Yeah right.") some continue to leap in and try to catch the wave. Unfortunately, to be successful you need to ride the property wave, not just catch the end of it. Most investments are long-term propositions.

The effect of properties being taken off the market combined with late and enthusiastic buyers into the market is that property prices can often continue to increase and arguably become over-valued. The news media will be full of people saying they can't believe the prices properties are going for, sellers are accused of being greedy, aspiring first home buyers become disgruntled and politicians will be pressured to "do something" about it. Although they are well-meaning, the market is going to soften at some point all by itself and anything politicians do in an attempt to "help" is likely to push the market into decline.

Flat period

If the government or central banks resist the urge to "do something" about the "property problem" then at some point factors will converge to slow down property price growth. The cycle and the market will then enter a generally flat period. Prices can, of course, either rise or fall a little during this period, however they generally remain flat. Individual locations can also rise and fall during this period.

The flat period (as opposed to a period of *falling* real property prices), usually occurs because a psychological barrier often prevents property prices falling. When a home owner with their house on the market has formed an opinion of what their property is worth, they are often very reluctant to sell it for less than that value. Sellers in this situation tend to view a lower sale amount as a *loss* — even if this lower amount is more (even much more) than they originally paid for the property. As most people selling don't *have to* sell their property, this psychological barrier is quite powerful.

During the flat period, other factors affecting the property market continue to change. While property prices stagnate, rental prices tend to increase which improves rental yields. Household incomes also rise while interest rates tend to fall.

Due to these changes, housing affordability gradually improves during the flat period, with the rate of improvement dependant on the level of economic changes … but these factors aren't regarded as particularly newsworthy hence not reported in the main media channels. Most people are unaware that these changes are occurring.

Eventually, property prices gradually become *undervalued* again. When a significant event occurs such as a rise in immigration, a surge of first home buyers, or even media reports claiming property prices are undervalued, conditions are ripe for large price increases.

Thus, the cycle continues, moving back into the growth phase. While the trend of the property cycle appears to be repetitive, the actual causes of the changes can differ — along with the size of their impact and duration. Mixed in with human nature, this is what makes accurate predictions of the property cycle so difficult in the short term.

However, just because it is difficult to predict the cycle in the short term, it doesn't mean there's no value in understanding the concept. Understanding the property cycle allows us to think in a more strategic manner, positioning ourselves to counter or take advantage of future market events rather than just dealing with what's happening in the present.

The property cycle also allows us to consider *change* and how we are going to prepare for that change in order to achieve our goals.

Strategies for different periods in the property cycle

Once property prices start to rise, then like a train they pick up momentum and can take a long time to slow down. This means that at the beginning of a growth cycle you can be reasonably confident of at least a few years of appreciating property prices. If you already own property, this capital growth increases your wealth and makes it easier to borrow further funds for further property purchases.

The growth (or recovery) period of the property cycle is probably the best time to take what you might perceive as a 'risk' in property. Risk is a relative word, meaning different things to different people. To some investors risk might mean buying two rental properties when they were only thinking about one. To others it may mean quitting their job, borrowing from friends or relatives and using credit cards to raise deposits on as many rental properties they can obtain and being a full-time investor. Whatever you judge as risk, make sure you have a *plan* and *analyse the numbers* carefully first. These two steps will reduce your exposure — no matter what your risk profile.

Irrespective of the part of the cycle in which you buy property, the general principle is that the more effort you put in, the better results you will achieve. Generally, ordinary properties provide ordinary returns, however with some effort you can greatly increase your return by adding value, increasing the rent, or negotiating a purchase price below market value. It is worth the effort.

Even in the early stages of a rising market, when you may be primarily anticipating property price increases, if you can improve your rental return and increase your cash flow you'll be able to acquire more property and do very well. Those who were motivated to buy a lot of property (and had the time, skills, and fortitude to do so) would have done very well between 2002 and 2005. Looking back you realise they couldn't really miss, but the difference between thinking about it and actually doing it is enormous. To take action at that point still takes courage.

Such a strategy isn't for everyone. In my experience, I find that most people do not want the stress that often comes with taking that investment approach. This is because most property investors have a full-time job and they have family or other commitments which also take up their time. Therefore they often don't have large amounts of time to pursue their investments. They also don't have an inclination to take on 'too much' risk. Yet in a rising market, this typical investor would have benefited from the relatively leisurely purchase of even a few ordinary rental properties. They would have done well — and without the worry of riskier strategies like buying up many properties and pushing their borrowing potential to the limit (and perhaps beyond).

During this period when property price growth exceeds rental price growth and interest rates increase, it's *essential* to achieve a good rental return to compensate for reduced cash flows. Buying well, adding value and adding features which allow you to increase the rental price become a *necessity* rather than just a method of maximising your return. It's also worth investing effort into locating potential property to buy — either directly or through building relationships with real estate agents. In a boom, agents are more concerned with *finding listings.* Properties practically sell themselves. Good luck with getting agents to call you with good property deals! Make sure you keep in touch with them. Talk to all agents, not just the 'good' ones. Often 'good' agents will be working hard for their vendor (to maximise the price) while less-experienced agents can be convinced to 'sell' your low offer to a vendor.

At the top of a boom many new and aspiring property investors conclude that it is too difficult to invest in property and so they withdraw from the market. More-experienced investors had stepped back from the market even earlier, realising that they faced too much competition to purchase property from other exuberant buyers, whether investors or first home buyers. Also in this period, experienced investors see agents use their offers to push up other buyer's bids.

Instead, experienced investors often review their existing rentals looking for ways to improve their returns — which is a very appropriate strategy for the future.

Strategies for the end of the boom

The period from the peak to the end of the boom can be the most difficult time in the cycle to buy an investment property. Rental yields are low, property prices are high and so are interest rates. After the boom period, these conditions continue for a time, but you don't have the benefit of rising property prices to make your investment work.

To operate effectively in these conditions, it can be a good idea to undertake more 'labour intensive' strategies such as:

- Adding bedrooms.

- Adding a minor dwelling.

- Building (even relocating) an extra house on a property you own if space and regulations will allow.

You should still *always* aim to pay a bargain price and make the best use of any existing structure by adding value through the economical and obvious means of paint, wallpaper, floor coverings, garden etc.

In a cooler market, bargain properties start to come onto the market when over-exuberant investors come under pressure. It may be they face changes in their funding arrangements, e.g. coming off lower fixed mortgage rates, and as a result are unable to fund their now heavily cash flow-negative rental property. For you as a buyer, it's a good strategy to maintain contacts with a wide network of real estate agents. If you do so, you'll find out about these troubled investors. Local property managers are also a potentially good source of information.

In order to assist these people with their 'problem', it's only fair that you should gain a good price in return. As a buyer, you need good negotiation skills and to be well-organised. Put yourself in the best position to help people out with selling their property and make the most of your strengths:

- You should have your finances organised.

- You don't have to sell a property in order to buy theirs.

- You can settle quickly or slowly depending on the nature of the seller's problem.

You *must* also be up-to-date with your market values so you can make a quick decision with confidence.

Most residential rental properties, even those in the provinces, purchased at the peak of the cycle will have a cash flow shortfall (even if you buy well and add value). If you are restricted to buying 'ordinary' property, this cash flow shortfall may be so great that it isn't worth buying the property as in the short to medium-term — you won't have market price increases to offset the cash flow losses. (If you can generate increased equity immediately, however, this can provide a counter benefit to any cash flow shortfall.)

A shortfall can also be offset with cash flow surpluses from your existing rental properties, or you may have sufficient income to confidently meet any shortfall. If you don't have other income, you can use a revolving credit facility (or a similar arrangement) and effectively capitalise your loan to offset the shortfall. This is a riskier option as your debt is increasing every year while your property value is static or possibly even falling. This reduces your equity, so you need to be confident that future increases in the property's value would cover the increasing debt.

Another way to reduce or eliminate cash flow shortfalls is to trade property and use the profits (hopefully) to reduce your borrowings on buy-and-hold rental properties. This requires buying the right property for the right price, good knowledge of the local property market, sound budgeting, and detailed project and time management. You must *know* what a property will be worth when you have either fixed it up or developed it, so you can budget the project cost and establish a purchase price which will include your profit margin. You should always allow for funding costs in your budget along with a contingency fund for project over-runs.

Trading is harder in a slow market as you will have fewer buyers to sell to and no market price increases to cover any mistakes you may make.

As the boom period ends and the flat period continues, investors in a sound financial position continue to pick the eyes out of the market. Although it can be difficult to get good cash flow from property purchased during the end of the boom period, if you *can* do it at this stage you will find it much easier later in the cycle.

Eventually market fundamentals change to the point where the market rallies. Two potential and significant changes are (1) rental price increases and (2) mortgage interest rate decreases. These can have a significant effect on your cash flow situation, potentially turning a negative cash flow property into a cash flow neutral or even positive property within a few years. The lower the initial cash flow deficit the more likely it is that this will occur, hence buying right in the first place is often critical.

As the fundamentals change, there will come a point where a market change event such as increased immigration or a flood of first home buyers will cause demand for property to outstrip demand and prices will rise. And so the cycle continues.

3

Different investors, different strategies

Andrew King

Just as there are different strategies for different periods of the property cycle, there are also different strategies for different investors. Property investors are usually described in the media as a homogenous group — and indeed, that's how we often talk about ourselves — but there are many different types of investors. They can be experienced or inexperienced, young or old, risk takers or risk-averse, those with a modest portfolio or substantial investors.

Let's examine a few different types of investor and consider strategies that may be useful for them to adopt during the flat or slump years of the property cycle. For simplicity, I will divide investors into three categories and discuss them under these headings: budding or unintentional investors; bullish investors; and old hand investors.

Budding and unintentional investors

Budding investors enthusiastically follow the market, read all the books and go to many seminars. They look at many investment properties for sale and they may know of people who have done very well out of property. They want a slice of the action for themselves … but they haven't done anything about it yet. *Unintentional investors* are those property investors who have either inherited a property or kept their old home as a 'rental' when they purchased a new home (in other words, the investment property wasn't a planned or conscious course of action.)

At the peak of a property cycle, investors need to have determination and commitment to source good property, enhance their investment and make it work.

In a slow market any shortfall in rental income is not offset (at the time) by capital gains. In fact a drop in value, should it occur, will reduce the return on the investment. Buying 'ordinary' property, i.e. property with no potential for added value or easily increased rental income, purchased at market value, does not make sense — it is likely to cost you a significant amount of money each month just to keep it afloat.

You could use a large deposit to reduce the amount of money required to fund the rental property. However, you may find that it is more worthwhile to keep the money in the bank earning interest and wait for conditions to become more favourable or until you can purchase better property that doesn't drain your resources so much.

If you're a budding investor determined to start investing in the slow part of the property cycle, then you may have to alter your strategy. Rather than buying 'ordinary' property it would be beneficial to look for property that you can add value to. Expect to increase the value of any property you purchase with the additional aim of improving the rental return. If you don't take this approach, you'll undoubtedly have to substantially support the investment financially, which will limit the amount of property you can purchase.

There are now mortgages that allow you to capitalise cash flow shortfalls back into the mortgage so that you don't have to make up the shortfall from your own income. Revolving credit mortgages can also be used for this purpose. This can work out well when property prices are rising, but it can also lead to your mortgage increasing while the value of your property remains the same or even decreases. This will lead to your equity reducing, which really isn't the point of investing in property.

If your equity falls far enough, your lender may decide to call in the loan which could have disastrous consequences.

Your strategy may be to purchase the property anticipating that rents will increase and mortgage interest rates will fall. This may be a reasonable assumption, but you need to consider the likelihood that this will occur and the level of change required to make your investment work.

Consider that you own a rental property valued at $300,000, renting for $300 per week with a 9.2% interest only mortgage on the full market value. It could cost you around $9,000 after tax each year to own this rental property.

In order for this rental to become cash flow neutral after tax, a combination such as interest rates falling to 7.2% and rents increasing by 20% needs to occur. This may be completely feasible; however you have to consider when these changes are likely to happen, as your capitalising mortgage will be increasing until this occurs.

Market conditions do not have to change as much for a property to become cash flow neutral if you purchased well and the property only costs you, say, $3,000 after tax to own.

This 'add value' path requires effort and sacrifice. If you're a budding investor, don't delude yourself (or believe the hype) that this is an easy way to become a millionaire by next Tuesday. Some property marketers, developers and property finders will try to make it sound easy — but if it was that easy, wouldn't everyone be doing it? Despite what you may have been told, they're not.

For those that have inherited a property or held onto an earlier home as a rental, your first step is to confirm that your old place is, in fact, a good rental property. Be warned: in many cases it isn't. Often people have a sentimental hold on the property or an unwillingness to pay an agent's fee to sell the place.

If you're going to be an investor, look at the property as an investment. What's the rental yield for the property? What's the cash flow it produces? Could you get a better return from another property, perhaps in a different area? Is there anything you could do to the property to improve the return — add a bedroom, renovate it, or add a feature desired by the target tenant group? If your old home doesn't meet the criteria for a good rental property then don't delude yourself. You may be better to sell it and buy one that is a better rental option.

It may be you have inherited a property (with a low or non-existent mortgage) and you believe that because of slow market conditions it isn't a good time to own investment property. You might even be tempted to sell it. In my view you should never sell a property without good reason, and that isn't a good reason.

If you have confirmed that it is a good rental and if the property is debt free, then you have a wonderful opportunity to use the equity and cash flow to purchase more rental property before the next growth phase of the property cycle.

Sometimes successful investing means forgoing income in the short term to allow you to purchase more property, and achieve a higher income in the long term. It isn't a 'this-or-that' decision of course. You could purchase a smaller number of properties and receive some income as well.

Despite being in a position to purchase ordinary property (defined earlier), there's no need to do it straight away. If you take your time to source bargain or properties with 'value-add' potential, for instance, you will be able to finance and buy more property over time. Additionally you will reduce your risk exposure through increasing your equity and cash flow.

If you have retained an older home after purchasing a new home, review the property as a rental — its appeal factors and shortcomings — and not as your old home.

This means looking at the property with a fresh pair of eyes. You may have loved the large garden of rose bushes, but are prospective tenants going to look after them? Could you add bedrooms to the property? (More bedrooms = wider appeal, more rental income.) Will your unique and spectacular decor appeal to the majority of tenants or only those discerning few who share your style preferences? You may not have needed a fenced section, but if your target tenants have young families, they will. Attending a meeting at your local property investors' association is a simple way to expand your knowledge on what makes a great rental property.

You should also ensure that you make the most of your tax and finance opportunities when retaining a previous home as a rental. Be prepared to consult a few suitably experienced and specialist professionals (i.e. don't necessarily use the same accountant for everything). Work to identify appropriate strategies for your individual circumstances.

Have you structured your borrowings to maximise your tax deductibility? Ideally you want to maximise your rental property mortgage payments (tax deductible) and minimise your personal mortgage payments (generally not tax deductible). If you still have a personal mortgage, it can be a good idea to make your rental property mortgage payments interest-only so that any cash flow goes into reducing personal debt before investment debt.

Make sure you know what the correct market rental price is for your rental property. Looking at comparable rental listings on Trade me is a good start as there are usually lots of photos which makes it easier to compare. However, the best method is to actually visit similar rental properties available for letting in your area. Many accidental rental property owners don't take the time to do this and lose thousands of dollars each year as a consequence.

Bullish new investors

Bullish new investors may already have some rental property or they may be keen to begin investing.

Back in 1998 bullish new investors would often call me with all their problems looking for solutions. Not only did interest rates rise and house prices fall in 1998, rental prices also fell due to a net population loss from migration. Typically, these bullish investors had bought two or three properties at or near the top of the market and now realised that they couldn't afford to hold them. Many were ordinary properties with little ability to have value added or an improved rental return.

Leading into a slow or flat market, investors who have already purchased a property or two would be well-advised to look dispassionately at their properties and the associated numbers — and see if their purchase was a wise move or not. At the height of the property cycle growth phase it may have seemed that upwards house prices and low interest rates would go on forever. But as the market changes, it's important to ask a couple of key questions:

1) Does my existing portfolio still fit in with my property goals?

2) If it doesn't, what type of property would?

Your answer to those questions may lead you to consider selling your existing rentals to purchase property that better fits in with your goals. Be open to this, but don't forget to factor in selling costs and the potential for future capital gains, as these may influence your decision.

Depending on how long ago you bought your rental property, and in what part of the cycle, you may or may not have seen your equity position increase. If you have maximised your borrowing capacity, or if you are concerned about your financial position facing a flat market, look for opportunities to increase your rental return and/or the property's value.

If you are a bullish investor, go back and read the section on budding investors and how to maximise your investment property. You're really in the same camp. The only difference is that you have already decided that you are willing to put in the effort to start investing. The benefit of investing in the lower part of the market cycle is that you will become 'battle-hardened'. If you can make investment property work in those circumstances, then future years will seem much easier.

Old hands

Investors who bought or have owned rental property prior to the growth phase of the cycle can feel pretty good. They've seen the value of their properties increase significantly and received a marginal improvement in their rental returns. But despite their increased net worth, their cash flow can still be poor.

Depending on their level of activity, these investors will often have high equity. However, yields tend to crumble in a boom — so their potential weakness is likely to be their ability to service debt. Facing the prospect of flat property prices over the short to medium-term and rental income that has not kept pace with previous years' house price growth, some old hands may consider selling property to reduce debt and avoid the drain on their cash flow. Others may consider this move so they can improve their debt servicing ratio and continue to purchase property — or replace properties they've sold with ones that provide a better return.

Some old hand investors may actually already be in a position to retire (or at least start taking an income from their rental property) and not even know it.

If you have had such a boost in equity through price increases over the boom period, you may be able to sell some of your rental properties and pay off the debt on the remaining properties. For many investors, three or four debt-free rental properties (income without the interest bill) could be all it takes to be financially independent.

I've met many investors who have worked hard for years building up a portfolio of properties. After reviewing their rental prices and confirming the true market value of their properties following a boom, many of these investors found themselves in a position to either retire or semi-retire.

If you're an old hand investor, you should analyse your current situation — you may be in a better position than you realise. Go through your portfolio and judge which properties are the best to keep and which you may consider selling. Compare the cash flow and ease of management of each property. Ideally you would keep the high-returning, easy to manage properties. Also take into account the likelihood of future capital gains for each property — if the property has reached its potential for capital gain in the meantime, it might be a better candidate for sale than one with obviously more 'upside'.

Analysing which property to sell and which to keep can often be a matter of judgement, as many of the positive aspects can oppose each other. For instance, a property providing the best rental return may be the hardest to manage.

Keeping yourself safe

If you bought good rental properties but were carried away by a gung-ho presenter at a seminar (which turned out to be a sales pitch) or a smooth-talking 'investment' salesperson, first look to keep yourself safe when the market and values fall. Try not to panic as things tighten up. Instead, focus on strengthening your position. You do not want to be forced to sell your property in that kind of market. Analyse your current situation and identify any risks you face. Be honest with yourself.

Interest rate changes

A trap that catches some out is when a low fixed-rate mortgage comes up for review. Be vigilant about your mortgages and know where you are with them. It's a good idea to keep a track of all borrowings in one place.

I use one spreadsheet document to hold information on all my loans and I recommend you do the same. Here are the column headings of my system which you may use or adapt to your own requirements.

- Property address
- Lender and account number
- Amount of loan
- Start date
- Interest rate
- Fixed rate term
- Fixed rate ends
- Comments

Using this simple table I can see at a glance when any of my loans are coming up for renewal and quickly calculate what the likely effect would be. When one of my fixed interest terms changes I copy and paste the previous details into another section of the spreadsheet so I can see what has happened with the loan over time.

If you are close to your financial limit, then being aware of your loan structure well in advance of any changes is essential. It is a good idea to remind yourself, six months in advance (put a note in your diary) that a fixed interest rate period is ending — this will give you plenty of time to deal with a potential problem.

Improving cash flow — some strategies

Cash flow is the life-blood of any business and keeping income and expenditure within your capabilities is essential. It may be that your net income drops in a flat market, requiring you to fund some investment property shortfalls. There are several steps you can take to improve cash flow, depending on the severity of the problem and the timeframe you have to find a solution.

1) Make sure you're charging market rents. As a landlord, you must keep up with the market rates — this entails a good degree of research. Increase your rents if this is justified.

2) Look at ways to improve your rental return. Would your tenants like (and be willing to pay for!) extra features such as a heat pump, carport, sleep-out etc. Ask them if there is anything extra they would like and how much extra rent they would be willing to pay for it. It's then a matter of working out if you can get an acceptable return for the extra investment.

3) Are there any other expenses that you could cut back on? This could include mowing the lawns or managing the property yourself. Importantly, think carefully before cutting back on expenses, especially maintenance. Deferred maintenance can lead to increased tenant damage and is off-putting to existing and potential tenants. Also remember when you do this, you're only *deferring* it, not eliminating it. You will have to spend this money at some point.

4) If your loan has both principle and interest components, consider extending the term of the loan or moving to paying interest-only. (If you have non tax-deductible debt you should really go for interest-only loans anyway, so you can use as much of your funds to pay down or reduce debt that's not tax-deductible.)

5) If you don't already have a revolving credit account, you could establish one to meet the extra interest costs (see earlier section on revolving credit). Using it to make up a cash flow shortfall ('capitalising' the extra interest) can be risky as anything other than a short term strategy. It can potentially reduce your equity if property prices remain flat. In the worst case, you could end up with insufficient equity and have the bank call in your loan or demand a lump sum reduction. (It can happen.)

6) Discuss options with your mortgage broker or bank lending staff. Your mortgage broker may be able to negotiate a lower interest rate for you or find another lender whose terms suit your circumstances better.

There may be other options you can take to either increase your income or decrease your expenses. For instance, consider getting a second job to increase your income and allow you to make the increased interest payments. If you have a larger home than you need, consider downsizing or renting it out and becoming a tenant yourself in a smaller property or in a less desirable area. A little short term hardship may actually help you and bring great benefit in the long term.

In my view, your last resort would be to sell a property you want to keep in order to reduce debt. If pressed, it's best to sell your more management-intensive, negative cash flow (but good equity) properties. (See the section on 'Old hands'.)

If you've reached the point where selling is your best option then you are better to come to terms with it and start the process sooner rather than later — and it's always much better to make your own decisions than to have the bank step in and make choices for you.

Profit from the downturn

At the top of the market cycle, property prices are at an all-time high, affordability is dismal and rental yields are at their lowest levels. When you move into the slowdown phase of the cycle you are still faced with these factors — but now you don't have the benefit of rampant property price increases.

At such a time it would be easy to get despondent and shrink into your shell or retreat; however, like most things in life, there is usually something good among the bad. In the case of a slowing property market there are two:

1) less competition from other buyers and

2) a higher proportion of people with property problems

A well organised investor with a long-term outlook can do very nicely while helping others with their problems. My advice to investors is to make sure you're making a profit from the day you buy each rental property.

Property investors make great buyers

Despite solutions being available for some property problems, unfortunately there will always be some people who, through ignorance, greed, poor decision making or just bad luck, will be forced to sell. As those who don't 'have to' sell will take their properties off the market, you'll actually find it *easier* to locate properties that you can purchase at a 'good' price in a downturn — there are proportionately more of them about.

As a property investor who has arranged your affairs to reduce the financial pressures you face, you are likely to be in a good position to help out these people who are having property difficulties. Your criteria are generally more flexible than your average home buyer's so it is easier for you to accommodate the seller's requirements. Property investors usually need fewer conditions than home buyers, so this reduces the seller's risk of a deal falling through when they are desperate for it to occur.

One of the greatest advantages for investors (and first home buyers) is that they generally don't have to sell an existing property in order to buy another. This takes away one of the major obstacles to a conditional sale going unconditional. By not needing to sell an existing property, investors reduce the risk to the vendor that the sale won't go through — and that's worth something.

As you're a property investor looking to buy, you should also have your mortgage finance established (or even prearranged) so you don't necessarily need a finance condition in the contract.*

* If there are no specific clauses for you to insert into the contract, consider a 'due diligence' clause which allows you a period of time to confirm your assumptions are correct and if not, to withdraw from the deal. (See *Property Law – A New Zealand Investor's Guide* for the wording of a good due diligence clause.)

Potentially one of the greatest benefits an investor can offer the troubled vendor is flexibility with the settlement date. Home buyers often fall in love with their new home and generally want to move in around a month after the sale goes unconditional. This may or may not suit the seller.

As an investor with no plans to live in the property, you can be more flexible regarding when settlement takes place. If it suits the seller to settle quickly, you can, if they want six months to move out, you can accept this. Whatever the seller wants, try to be flexible.

As an investor you should be as flexible as possible in many ways except one: price. In return for making it easier for the seller, you need to be compensated — usually by buying the property at a good price. This is *especially* important in a flat market.

Adding value — do your sums

As well as aiming to buy at a bargain price, look for ways to add value to a property — and this doesn't just mean blindly spending money on it! Over-capitalisation is a sin! If all you do is increase the value of the property by the cost of the improvements, that's pointless (unless you achieve higher rent). Aim to add much *more* value to the property than the improvements cost you.

The classic do-up is probably your best bet. A good rule of thumb is that you should aim to increase the value of the property by three or four dollars for every dollar you spend. This starts with buying the right property. If you're aiming to use this do-up strategy, make sure you start with the houses that require only *cosmetic improvements* — not structural work.

By focusing on cosmetic issues — the surface — you can make a significant and perceivable difference to the value of the property.

As a general rule, if the items that need repairing are mostly visible, it is probably a good do-up property. (But be careful with kitchens: the layout should be workable and cabinets should not need replacing.) Generally, if it seems as if the house needs work on too many of its 'invisible' items e.g. electrical wiring, plumbing, foundation work, it may not be a good do-up candidate. Those improvements cost money but don't tend to add value in the eyes of a valuer or purchaser.

There may be features you can add to the property which are both desirable to tenants and add value to the property. Some examples are a garage or carport, fencing, or a storage shed. Think of what the tenants would want. Again, be flexible. At the start, you may need to put in your own labour or buy second-hand items to make the project work. Talking to other members of your local Property Investors Association is a great way to hear how others have economically added value to their properties.

One member of the Auckland association I spoke to started his investing in 1998. This was a time when newspaper headlines screamed 'Don't invest in property!' Nevertheless, over four years this investor purchased eight do-up properties, in each case buying well and adding value. He borrowed against the equity in his own home to make his purchases with 100% finance, then refinanced each property as the improvements were completed. Rising rents over the four years helped him along. By 2002 he had doubled his starting equity and a few years into the growth period had equity of over $2 million.

Developing and trading in a slump

Developing can be a successful way to add tremendous value to a property. It could involve adding a minor dwelling, or building a new dwelling on the back section of an existing property, or perhaps building or moving a house onto a section.

Trading can be much more difficult during a slowdown compared to the growth stage of the property cycle as the market will not conceal any mistakes you make, such as cost over-runs. If you are relying on these developing activities as your source of income then it can be risky, to say the least. Only do it with a good deal of planning and caution. *(see Mike McCombie's section on development – ed.)*

If you are successful at adding value to property, you may consider trading some property as a way of providing income or to reduce your borrowing on property you choose to keep. There are many tax issues regarding trading and you need to ensure your trading activities do not 'taint' your buy-and-hold rental properties.

It is absolutely *essential* to get good advice from an accountant knowledgeable in property before you start this type of activity. The laws around these areas are changing — e.g. changes to the Associated Person rules (covering 'tainting') — and these could restrict your options.

Also go carefully if you are considering trading. Cost over-runs combined with a slowing market can blow out your holding costs and quickly wipe out your planned margins. Don't go into this without a great deal of relevant knowledge and make sure you plan well.

If you approach the project correctly, then generally the more you can do to a property, the better your return will be — and the lower your risk. Cash flow is one of the most pressing issues for investors following a boom. It is a lack of cash flow which gets in the way of many investors who would like to finance more property purchases. Aiming for a higher return with both equity and rental income helps put you in a better position to buy more property.

Investing in other locations

If you cannot add value to property, it may benefit you to consider buying rental property in areas where average rental yields are higher. Take care to avoid costly mistakes when investing in unfamiliar territory. One way to do this is to thoroughly research that target area so that you are comprehensively aware of factors such as:

- Market values.

- Achievable rental returns.

- Desirable and less desirable locations.

- Target tenant groups and their needs.

- The outlook for the local economy.

Use caution when you consider buying property in 'rough' areas because of the higher rental return these areas often provide. This return is high for good reasons: increased costs in management, tenant damage, and rent arrears. These can quickly erode an initially attractive rental yield and cause a lot of anguish.

There are other aspects to consider. Sometimes 'high yielding' locations can expose you to higher expenses such as insurance, rates, repairs and maintenance — these can consume a higher percentage of the rental return when compared to other lower yielding areas.

For these reasons, make sure you carefully calculate a budget for the property. Look at the cash flow it produces — not just the gross rental yield.

Know your market

Whatever you plan to do to add value to a property, up-to-date market knowledge is the key to success. Before you start a project, you need to know what the value of the property will be when the project is complete. Using that projected value, you can work backwards, factoring in the cost of the project (and allowing your profit margin!) to determine what the property is worth to you.

As with all business projects, research, planning and well-organised implementation are the keys to success. There is no better way to get to know an area than to go to as many open homes as possible — view and analyse the numbers on as many properties as you can. This provides essential and up-to-date information on the market, and gives you a sound knowledge of the area including its good and bad parts, where the tenant areas are and local amenities.

In addition to knowing the property market, you *must* know the rental market as well. Armed with this information you will be more efficient looking for property and better able to make fast buying decisions.

Don't lose heart — the market is always changing

If all your plans and strategies still don't produce the results you want, remember, nothing lasts forever. The factors influencing the market (house prices, rental prices, affordability, interest rates etc) are continually changing. At the peak of the property cycle these factors tend to move in a direction that makes it difficult to provide rental accommodation. During the slowdown period of the cycle, however, the trend changes. These same factors start moving, however slowly, in a direction that makes the market a little easier for investors. At some time in the cycle, conditions are likely to emerge which will make cash flows easier again and increase the upwards pressure on property prices.

Although you may not be in a position to purchase as many properties as you would like at any one time due to market conditions, don't let this stop you from investing altogether. Don't be negative. Just as I've advised you to consider the effect of the 'negative' market changes — factors such as interest rates and rental prices — I also suggest that when you're in the market to buy a property, you look on the other side of the coin. Consider the positive pressures as well. The market is always changing.

Play with the numbers

What would the impact be on a property that you purchase today if interest rates fall by, say, 2%? Or what if rents increased by 20% over the next two or three years?

- A fall in interest rates by 2% (say 9.5% to 7.5%) will increase the cash flow on a $300,000 loan by $6,000 a year.

- A 20% increase in rental prices for a $300 per week rental property would increase cash flow by $3,000 a year.

How would this affect your cash flow? Of course you can't make these market changes happen, but as an investor, if you're familiar with the effect of those trends, you can watch the market as these and other fundamentals trend in your favour — and they may influence your timing and your purchase decisions.

When making predictions and assumptions on how the market will change over the next few years, try to be balanced and reasonable. Don't assume everything is going to be positive if there are not good reasons to expect this. Likewise, don't assume everything is going to be negative if it isn't likely. Relentlessly negative thinking will prevent you from taking action.

Last word: Making it at the sharp end of the cycle

Property prices have always gone through cycles and this is likely to continue into the future. Although previous cycles are no guarantee of how future cycles will evolve, the general pattern of the cycles is fairly well established. I think it is fair to rely on things continuing in that pattern — despite some self-interested sales hype to the contrary.

Certainly, property prices are relatively stable compared to share prices. Why? Because it takes longer to sell a property, the value of the asset is subjective, and the majority of properties are held by home owners rather than investors.

Most home owners do not 'have to' sell their property and this tends to provide a barrier to property prices falling. If vendors cannot get what they believe their property is worth they simply don't sell. This means that a decline in the property market primarily reduces the number of properties sold but does not, in general, lead to across the board price reductions.

Despite average property prices being relatively protected, individuals can still be negatively affected to significant degrees, and some may lose everything during the decline period of the property cycle. Those most at risk are investors who have over-leveraged themselves and anyone who is in a position where they have no other option but to sell their property.

My first advice to investors under pressure is to try not to panic. Next, assess and address problem areas in your investments. If you can't identify a strategy to protect your current position, consider selling property while you still have some control — rather than have the decision taken out your hands by your lender.

There is no doubt that some investors will not survive the downturn. Other investors will be only too willing to take their property off the hands of those who are struggling — at prices that make financial sense for the buyer. That's just how it works.

The peak of the property cycle can be one of the toughest times to purchase investment property. Cash flow is generally poor and there is unlikely to be any capital growth in the short to medium term to counter negative earnings. It is unlikely that purchasing 'ordinary' property will be a good investment for many investors. In this situation, my advice is to apply your focus to purchasing property at a discount to market value, and looking for ways to add value to both the property and the rental income.

Although it is difficult to purchase investment property with sound fundamentals at the peak of the cycle, those who do so tend to be disciplined, and this can lead to developing good purchasing practices. In general, if you can purchase good investment property then you can probably do it at any point.

Every property investor is different, with different goals, strengths and weaknesses. Each one is in charge of their own business. Aim to learn from the past, plan for the future, and act in the present with diligence. Do this and you will be on your way to achieving the outcomes you desire.

I wish you all the best with your investments.

Andrew King is the co-author of *The Complete Guide to Residential Property Investment in New Zealand* and author of *Planning for Property Success*. See recommended reading.

4

An introduction to cycles

Mike McCombie

When reflecting on business or investing, it can be useful to observe the natural world. Have you ever noticed that nature is constantly changing? Nothing stays the same for very long. Living things are always expanding or shrinking, rising or falling, growing or dying. This almost continuous change can appear to be random, but in many cases the variations are governed (or at least influenced) by underlying natural rhythms — patterns and cycles.

We breathe in and breathe out, for example. This is known as 'the respiratory cycle' a relatively short cycle that takes place during our lifetimes. We may not always be conscious of it, but this cycle consists of two phases: *expansion* (inhale), and *contraction* (exhale). In addition, ideally there's a *pause*, however short, between each phase of the cycle.

Throughout the respiratory cycle there are 'triggers', such as oxygen and carbon dioxide levels in our blood, that tell our body when to breathe in; when to pause; and when to exhale. There are also factors that influence the length and speed of our inhalations and exhalations — such as our level of physical activity (how demanding it is), or our emotional state.

We can extend the inhalation or the exhalation or the pauses, holding our breath even until we're blue in the face, yet eventually the cycle carries on. We breathe in, we breathe out.

Consider another example: the digestive cycle. We eat (expand), digest (pause) and excrete (contract). Notice again, ideally there is a pause between each stage of the cycle — in fact our digestive system works considerably better when these pauses are taken.

Consider the first meal of the day: it's called 'break-fast'. It's natural for there to be a pause, a period of rest or fasting, between meals. After the pause we eat again. Can you spot the pattern? Expansion–pause–contraction. This is a common pattern with cycles which are happening as things constantly change around us.

Some situations and circumstances can change very quickly, in a heartbeat, because their cycle is very short or the change is triggered by some external event such as an earthquake or tsunami. Other changes, such as the weather, occur in hours, days or months. Still other changes can occur very slowly, even taking years in the case of climate change, or hundreds of years, even millions of years for geological changes.

We may not notice the change and often we don't. However, minute by minute, day by day, or even month by month things change. We can get used to a certain state, to life being the way it is, and we can easily think it will either *always* be like this, or at least be stable for a long time. Yet change continues.

Another interesting factor is that as people affected by change and cycles, we seem to *prefer* certain parts of the cycle over others. Staying with the digestive example, we go out to dinner parties with our friends and have a few drinks and something to eat. We tell people about the fantastic meal we had, often in great detail, morsel by morsel. But whoever heard of excretion or elimination parties? We don't celebrate this part of the cycle, although it is a critical part of the process. (I've done a few fasts and various associated activities like colonic cleanses which I won't describe here, yet I've noticed when I start to talk about them people definitely don't want too much detail!)

So even though we don't luxuriate and dwell on the elimination phase it is really important, in fact it is *critical* to our physical well-being. The contraction phase rids the body of the waste generated during the consumption and digestive phases of the cycle. It cleans the system. As you read this book, I hope you'll come to see that property and economic cycles are also cyclical. The contraction phase plays as important a role as the other parts of the cycle. I've come to realise that all of the parts of the cycle are necessary. One or other part of the cycle is not 'wrong' or 'bad', positive or negative, it just *is!* Each part is important and useful.

Adjusting to the season

> There is no such thing as bad weather
> Only bad clothes.
>
> — Hermann Gieck

Let's look at the weather more closely. I'm sure you'll agree it's normal to change our behaviour with the seasons. Consider how we behave differently at different times of the year.

In winter, for example, the weather can be extremely cold. In response to this situation we change how we dress — piling on warm protective clothes — and how we work and play. People hibernate more, eat more comfort food, stay inside and sit by the fire during the cold season. Their winter and summer rhythms are significantly different.

For many people, winter leisure pursuits include skiing, or alpine adventuring or mountain climbing. Some of the most adventurous go out into extreme conditions — into circumstances they would normally avoid, for adventure, but they prepare very well (failure to do so would be perilous).

By contrast, in the summer time, when the weather is fine (to use the immortal words of Mungo Jerry) most people don't go snow skiing — they go water skiing! Instead of alpine and snow clothing, they hardly wear any clothes. Half-naked, they relax on the sand, go swimming in the water or get pulled around on top of it, buzzing around behind a speed boat — all in pursuit of a 'great time'. It would be considered abnormal, insane, in the middle of summer to load up your ski gear, head for the mountains and try to ski down the slopes — there's no snow! It would be equally insane to go swimming in the sea in the middle of an icy winter (although some people do it, albeit briefly).

To summarise, given a change in season we change our behaviour, modify our clothing and equipment — and our definition of 'fun'. (We also *prepare* for a change in season, *before* it happens, but more on that later.)

My point is, it is normal for us to change *what we do* and *how we do it* in the various cycles and seasons. It is normal to operate under a different set of rules depending on the season. We don't bother trying to make summer or winter 'wrong', or to waste time arguing that it will or won't happen, we just prepare and adjust. The same rules and logics apply with business and investing.

Business people spend time analysing patterns and cycles so that they can understand the implications and consequences of these patterns. The goal is to be able to forecast future changes with some accuracy, in order to plan and adapt our behaviour(s) to those changes. The aim is to protect ourselves from the dangers, risks, and harsh aspects of these cycles and changes and enjoy the benefits of them.

Property investing is no different.

Changing strategies

In terms of their economic choices some people develop just *one* strategy and try to apply that to any and every situation. We don't do this in any of the examples I've given you. As the weather cycle alters, we respond by changing our clothing. Similarly, as we age, we alter our behaviour(s) to suit our levels of age, health, well-being and confidence. We learn to understand and respect the different rhythms of life. But some people affected by the economic cycle seem to try to ignore it and continue to do the same thing.

For instance, a property investor might say, 'I just buy, borrow as much as I can, and hold' or 'I'm just a developer' or 'All I do is trade'. When the cycle changes, these people can be adversely affected in significant ways because their actions no longer fit the current part of the cycle. What they successfully did before no longer works. A behaviour that was successful in one part of the cycle can fail miserably or be disastrous in another part of the cycle. They can get burnt.

This fact is evident when we consider investment paradigms from the past. For most of the last 75 years, successful investing meant a strategy of buying property, borrowing as much as possible against the property (often with high gearing ratios), and sitting back and watching the equity grow. The benefits of this system were that you received a good return, not just on the *cash* you invested but on the *value* of the whole property. Leverage was your friend — the more the better.

In a falling property market it isn't property investment itself that becomes the problem, but rather excessive borrowings. Leverage is no longer beneficial when values fall or slump.

Another example is found in building conversions. There's a time to convert a city-fringe warehouses into office space (because there's a shortage of office space) — and there is a time when an *oversupply* of office space, or excessive upgrade or purchase costs, make that a far more risky endeavour.

To illustrate, let me tell you my experience in the 1980s. I prospered in the early '80s buying vacant property when the market was improving and seemed to be going into a very strong phase. I had spare cash flow and I found tenants quickly, added value to the vacant properties by leasing them … and made good profits. Yet when I tried this same strategy to try to get out of a financial tight spot in the *late* '80s, after the market had turned, I ran into significant problems.

I bought a couple of vacant unit-titled warehouses on Old Hutt Road in Lower Hutt, at what would have been a good price when the market was buoyant. But the market had turned. Capitalization rates had increased (meaning values dropped — see explanation in Chapter 6), banks wouldn't lend as much on vacant properties … and as hard as I tried, I just couldn't find any tenants. So instead of making money (as I had in the past) I was forced to sell the vacant property, still vacant, at an even lower price than I had paid for it and dug myself into a deeper hole. Timing is everything.

Understanding and predicting change

History may not always repeat, but it does rhyme.

— Mark Twain

Your job (in life, and as an investor) is to develop a *range* of strategies that you can use in different circumstances, during different parts of a cycle. It is a fact of life that some activities will work better at different times, because they will 'fit' the cycle better.

There is immense value in gaining some understanding of cycles. If you can master the art of using the past to help predict the future, this knowledge will assist you in setting up your life so it works better — and you will not only survive, but prosper.

Although there are no guarantees that the past will exactly repeat, by analysing past patterns you *can* gain insight into the market and an element of probability about what might happen in the future. As I write this, I've been a property investor for almost thirty years. During that time I have seen the property market rise and fall a number of times. It never remains the same for long. This continual change presents huge *opportunities* and *challenges* to the investor.

If managed well, these market changes can see you as an investor not just stay safe but also prosper greatly. If the changes are *not* managed well, financial stress (even ruin) can result.

To reiterate, a falling, contracting property market is *not* 'bad' or 'wrong' — it just is. This same market can provide massive opportunities. I've made some of my best deals and easiest money by buying well in falling or fallen markets. Yet I've also made stupid mistakes, lost millions and was even once bankrupted by not being aware and not properly understanding the changing market.

Throughout the next few chapters of this book, I will share my understanding of how the property market works, and my knowledge about cycles and their implications. I'll share my insights, hard lessons learned, and strategies so you cannot only avoid the dangers of a falling property market (and the pain of being crunched by it) but hopefully prosper and profit from it.

Summary

Re-capping factors to consider in relation to economic and property cycles...

All is changing. We may not notice the change, yet the change still occurs.

The change is not random. It's governed by rhythms and cycles. Some cycles are short term — some are very long term.

These cycles involve *expansion, pause, contraction*.

There are triggers that instigate change. It can be useful to identify these and stay aware of them and the trends.

Understand that factors influence, extend or cut short the length of the parts of the cycle.

We experience different parts of the cycle differently, enjoying expansion and finding the contraction phase more challenging.

Despite our differing appreciation of them, no phase is right or wrong, good or bad — they're just different and serve important functions.

It is useful, even necessary, to modify our actions to suit our situation in the current cycle, and where we may be going.

A key is to analyse the past and present, to forecast the future, to protect ourselves from the harsh aspects of the cycle — and make the most of the benefits.

Be prepared early.

As we'll see, another investing key is to retain *control*.

5

The Market

Mike McCombie

What is the 'property market'?

In simple terms, 'the market' is what people (owner-occupiers, investors, investment companies, family trusts and other entities) are willing to buy and sell property for. The market is simply the sum of the decisions these various interests make — what the group or 'the crowd' decides about the current value of property.

Incidentally, when I was a less experienced investor I used to believe a registered valuer would tell me *the value of a property*, you know, *the* value — definitively, conclusively, and that I could rely on that information. I now understand that valuers are just part of this system and that their estimate is merely a report on the value of a property at a set point in time with the prevailing market conditions. They simply look at the latest sales or leasing evidence and report on it. So to a large extent they are just reporting on the crowd view — and actually in 'lag' or out-of-date to the extent of the delay in them getting up-to-date information on sales and lease agreements.

The market reflects what these groups are willing to buy, sell or lease their properties for — not just the values and prices, but also the terms and conditions they want and how long they're willing to wait for a suitable deal. Notably, these conditions and terms are sometimes *more important* than price. Often when the market has fallen or slumped there is huge scope for creativity with terms and conditions. You can get terms which you just won't be able to negotiate in a strong market e.g. vendor finance, delayed settlement, access to renovate, trades as part or full payment and all manner of help from the vendor that you would not get when the market is booming.

These factors are determined by this group behaviour or belief. Sometimes this group (the market) values property higher, predicts prices only increasing and thus only wants to sell at very high values. At other times the group discounts the value because it thinks that property is of little value, or it sees values are decreasing and buyers are scarce (i.e. it is not 'flavour of the month' and few want to buy it). The market is driven as much by emotion as it is by economic fundamentals and trends.

Meet Mr Market

In *The Winning Investment Habits of Warren Buffett and George Soros* (see recommended reading) author Mark Tier relates how investor Warren Buffett's mentor Benjamin Graham coined the term 'Mr Market' to refer to the market. Mr Market is essentially a psychotic who sometimes values his assets incredibly highly — holding an unrealistically high perception of what his assets are worth. At other times Mr Market acts like a manic depressive who suddenly despises his assets and wants to be rid of them, selling them at ridiculously low prices.

Graham's operating beliefs were that (1) Mr Market is *always wrong* and (2) the wonderful thing is that you do not have to do what the market says. The market is passive. It puts assets up for sale at these ridiculous prices (whether high or low) and investors have the *choice* to buy them or not.

The good thing is that most of the time we (as owners, investors, buyers and sellers) can choose when we enter this market and whether we want to sell or buy into it... or wait until the time is best for us. Whatever the market puts up for sale, in normal circumstances there is nothing forcing us to buy it. In fact, when the market is maniacally high, we probably don't want to buy, but may want to sell. My easiest and most fruitful deals have been done by buying and selling in the opposite direction to the market trend — against the prevailing market mood.

This may be one of the most critical points for any investor or property owner. We must set ourselves up so that we can play the game *when* and *how* we want. I call this the aspect of *control*.

We choose when we buy and sell. We do not have our timing dictated by the market. We avoid situations such as having to sell into a low market because of pressure resulting from poor decisions we've made. The aim is to set yourself up so you can choose when you enter the market — whether you buy, sell, or sit in a market. *Get that control.* If you truly understand this and set yourself up accordingly, you will not be one of the victims of the next correction but will instead be ready to make phenomenal gains.

So, having established (1) the property market is constantly changing and (2) this change is often cyclical, let's take a closer look at cycles.

Economic cycles

The economy regularly goes through economic cycles from so-called 'boom' times to 'busts' or 'slumps'. These are caused by the interplay between supply and demand — and how parties respond to them. In New Zealand, where the economy is fairly small, the cycles vary in length and average around five to seven years for the general economy. Larger economies such as Australia and America tend to have longer cycles. The cycles also vary in severity, ranging from a mild and gradual correction to a sharp and severe drop.

A *recession* is defined as when the GDP (Gross Domestic Product — a measurement of economic growth) is negative for three or more consecutive quarters. A *depression* is a very severe and long lasting correction in the economy and subsequent asset prices.

There is also a school of thought that the boom and bust cycles of the past have been replaced by the 'bubble' cycle. This is an even more extreme fluctuation of the economy where a boom keeps expanding — going longer and higher until an asset bubble is created. This is followed by a major correction when the bubble 'pops'. This theory also holds that governments (through national or federal agencies including central banks) try to 'manage' or regulate the economy's boom and bust cycle. Basically, they use financial controls such as interest rates or levers in the money supply to try to affect the markets, control inflation and the economy. Often their aim is to try to avoid or minimise the extremes of the cycle. In situations of this kind, governments may attempt to avoid a recession or a depression by engineering aspects of the cycle; they may create, for example, a 'soft landing' in the down part of a cycle, loosening financial constraints. Or sometimes they try to dampen down a market that they believe is expanding too fast, or a boom that in their judgement has carried on for too long. Federal reserves and central banks adjust factors such as liquidity, credit controls, the cash supply and interest rates to tweak the economy. These factors all have an affect on asset prices, including property.

Some people believe that government intervention like this *never* works — that the officials always get it wrong, either through misjudging the timing or because fiscal controls are abused due to political agendas, election timing etc. In fact, many proponents of this theory say the government's actions actually *intensify* asset value bubbles — which always eventually pop. (External forces can pop these bubbles or the government or central bank initiates actions to pop them.)

As I've already stated, I believe that no part of the cycle is in itself wrong or 'bad' — it just is. The downward or descending part of the economic cycle, which is often viewed negatively or with some trepidation, is very important, as it cleanses or eliminates waste. Look at what happened in the US with Enron and other examples of corporate abuse built up through the expansion cycle. (This waste is not uncommon in the expansion phase of a cycle where operators using lax practices are often cushioned from the full impact of their actions by a rising market.) Also, look at the global 'credit crunch' caused in the US sub-prime mortgage market following the lax lending practices in that sector. Billions of dollars were lost by lenders, and thousands of mortgages were foreclosed as the results of lax lending practises were revealed. As the market turns, this sort of behaviour is increasingly exposed and forcibly cleaned up. This is illustrated very well by the following quote:

> It's only when the tide goes out that you learn who's been swimming naked.
>
> — Warren Buffett

We do not see who is exposed until after the market changes. There are always those operators (cowboys) who like to push the boundaries, take short-cuts and/or stretch themselves to the limit. (I used to be one of these operators and I was a casualty of the 1987 crash.)

When I look at this experience closely I think there were two major factors that led to my downfall, namely *ignorance* and *greed*. I was ignorant of how the market could behave in a downturn. I had never experienced it. In NZ and Australia today there are many younger investors in the same boat. For the last twenty years they have experienced essentially even sailing and relentless growth; any setbacks have been fairly shallow and short-lived.

This ignorance, coupled with my greed, saw me continually moving from one deal to the next in an attempt to acquire more and more, constantly raising the stakes. I had an attitude of 'do it all *today*' rather than relaxing a little and taking things a little more slowly, or ensuring a deal was properly settled before taking another step.

So if this describes you and you find yourself stretched in an upbeat, positive market, be warned, because the pressure will only increase, from all manner of directions, when the market turns.

What happens is that a 'contraction' comes through the market and it cleans out people and companies who haven't been operating effectively and efficiently. Thus, the downside provides a very useful function — although a very painful one — for those caught up in it.

Many people, for example, have been chasing yields as the market strengthened and yields on prime assets dropped (meaning prices rise in relation to income). To get their desired yield they may have invested in more and more risky deals or areas without a safety buffer. These investors are always at risk when the market tightens up (see the chapter, *What can go wrong?*) because a contraction usually sees risky and fringe investments affected more.

In the US and around most of the world since the 1990s, there has been a huge run in asset prices — and not just property. Shares, commodities and a range of other financial and non-financial assets seemed to be increasing at the same time. In the past these various classes have experienced growth at different times.

So there may be cause for concern about what happens when that particular bubble bursts. I don't mean to scare you (or maybe I do!) but we could have a global major correction in asset values looming — including property.

Long term cycles

Some also believe these short term economic cycles are part of a longer term economic cycle of about 75 years' duration. (For more detail, search the internet for 'Elliott Wave Theory').

This theory suggests that you start, or end with a depression — depending on where you want to start in the cycle. This long term cycle is characterised by a build up in asset values over time, with a number of smaller cycles running throughout the major 75 year cycle, then another depression or major correction... and the cycle begins again.

The last depression (they still call it the 'Great Depression') was in 1930.

How it could play out — a 75 year cycle

After the Great Depression asset prices where extremely low because Mr Market (remember him?) was feeling very depressed. He didn't even want to get out of bed to do anything. The value of assets had crashed. People who made the decision to buy following the Depression bought because they could see there were *fundamentally undervalued* assets for sale — greatly undervalued based on their fundamentals.

The market experienced growth (see graph below) ① there was some profit-taking and the market corrected downwards. Later, the market rose again ② (because the assets were still undervalued), and again there was another correction. Then there was a third cycle of increase ③ as some assets were still providing solid value and opportunity for growth. Another correction came along, followed by a fourth boom ④ motivated by momentum from the earlier rises. However, at this stage the fundamentals no longer justified the increase. Then there was another correction. Finally (and here the theory is making predictions) the *fifth* cycle comes around ⑤, and the market rises again before a major correction or crash in asset values. The last cycle rise, according to the theory, is funded by credit expansion! (*Sound familiar?*)

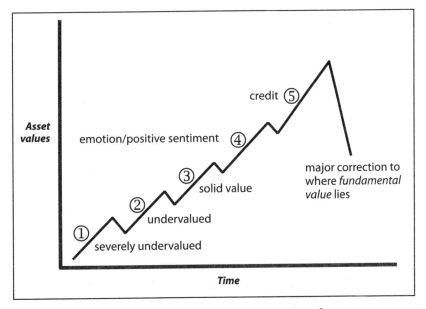

Figure 5.1 *Graph of long term (75 year) cycle*

During this last credit-fuelled boom, borrowing money is no problem — in fact it is easy to obtain credit. After this last expansion, the theory predicts the market drops to about the level of the third cycle of increase because that is where the fundamentals were. (For more detail on Elliott Wave Theory, see Robert Prechter's book *Conquer the Crash* in recommended reading.)

My experience of the last few years is that there has been an unprecedented increase in the availability of credit — to individuals, corporates and even governments). Household debt (comprising mortgages, credit cards and personal loans) is at record highs. Lending criteria has been increasingly loosened: There's been a boom in lending on no deposit, 100%+ loans, with no proof of income (lo-doc and no-doc loans or 'liar's loans'), more and more lending advanced on increasingly easy terms and conditions.

One of the media buzz phrases is 'mortgage stress', a term which describes those who are committing more than 40% of their income to mortgage costs.

In the US, the sub-prime mortgage sector and the associated lending entities are under huge pressure from defaulting loans and falling house values. These lenders target higher risk borrowers with poor credit ratings, or low or no deposit (i.e. 100% finance or close to it). The pressure caused by defaulters is now starting to spread into a range of financial institutions around the world who have purchased groups of these assets (the dreaded 'Consolidated Debt Obligations').

The central banks of a number of economies have been forced to inject money into their banking systems to try to avoid a credit squeeze. At the time of writing, the bad loans still exist and banks and financial institutions have yet to revalue their books to reflect the decreased value of their assets. Now that the idyllic part of the lending cycle (and the party) is over, lenders are looking for strategies to avoid the fallout of their lending binge. (As Warren Buffett says, "Dumb lending always has its consequences.")

Hedge funds, no more?

Another phenomenon is the huge growth, and fundamental change of operations, for many of the world's hedge funds. In the past, these investment funds were primarily used to manage risk such as foreign exchange risk or profit from taking a contrasting market position to the norm. Their *raison d'être* has been to take a counter-cyclical position on whatever slice of the global market they focused on.

Now, however, hedge funds have been used to effectively place open bets on how a currency, or commodity, or a wide range of other transactions may perform. Again, their popularity has been boosted by the worldwide search for higher yields. Money has poured into them. So a large number of them have become essentially *speculative* funds. The hedge fund market is huge. One recent estimate put the size of the total hedge market as *ten times* the value of the actual global economy.

Imagine if all these 'bets' were called in! Such a contraction could have a phenomenal impact on world markets, causing a major downwards correction in asset values.

Governments have not been immune to this credit expansion either. They have been increasing the money supply by printing more money. This has resulted in a reduction of the *value* of money and has helped push asset prices increasingly higher. It used to mean something to be a millionaire, to have a net worth of a million dollars. Now, according to a recent definition in *Forbes* magazine, you are not considered rich unless you have an *income* of a million dollars a year!

In summary, we have just been through a sustained and long period of asset value growth supported by a huge growth in credit.

A number of commentators have stated that we are overdue for a correction. Others say that this time, it's 'different'.

Who knows if we are overdue or not? A review of past patterns and cycles suggests that there *will* be a correction at some stage. This same analysis also suggests that the longer and bigger the upside, the deeper and more severe will be the downwards correction.

Do we know the exact timing and extent of this expected correction? No. But do I believe there will be a correction? Yes. I don't think it would take much for it to be an immensely significant correction with very real implications for investors and home owners alike.

In my experience, what tends to happen is that the market changes over time, fundamentals go increasingly awry, slipping out of whack, then there comes a time when there is lots of 'noise' along the lines of: 'Will-it-or-won't-it correct?', and then some event happens which acts as a trigger, the impact of which spreads incredibly quickly. Significant numbers of people will be caught — and afterwards many will say (with the benefit of hindsight) "Oh yeah. We knew it couldn't carry on like that. It was only a matter of time."

No-one ever loses money in hindsight.

The deniers: 'It's different this time.'

We are totally surrounded by cycles — yet some commentators and economists suggest the idea of an economic cycle has lost relevance. They say previous cycles are a thing of the past. Because we have computers now that have computerised inventory, to avoid supply imbalances, or we have improved forecasting techniques, or thanks to the Reserve Bank Act, or Treasury, we've conquered inflation, etc. Still others say fundamentals have changed, we've reached a new plateau and it is different this time. They cite reasons such as the global economy or the European Union or Australian pension funds or NZ superannuation funds or Kiwisaver etc. Honestly, I've lost track of how many times I've heard "It's different this time" before!

I don't believe it. "It's different this time" is a fallacy. In my experience night follows day, contraction follows expansion, a slump follows a boom which follows a slump. The market will always 'correct'. Therefore, if at any given time the market is high (i.e. above its trend line), in my experience it is due for a correction — downwards. Conversely, if the market is low, then in my opinion, an upwards correction is imminent.

There is always a lot of noise about the market. Will it go up more? Will it stay down? People expound on why it is different this time, why a 'crash' is imminent, why it isn't! All of these often opposing views jostle for attention in the marketplace.

As I've said, we often *do not know* until after the event. Hindsight is a wonderful thing. The economy will change and is always changing. Be prepared. Here it comes.

Risk — a more useful question to ask

So, rather than asking the futile questions — such as whether it will or won't go up, down, sideways etc — some more useful questions to ask could be these: If a recession, or a depression or even a major correction occurs:

1) Can I survive?

2) How could I prosper?

Also, it is *never* too early to ask yourself:

3) What are my weak points?

4) Where am I exposed to risk?

It may be, for example, that you have good assets with a lot of equity, but poor cash flow. Perhaps you should consider whether selling some assets to reduce your debt will strengthen your cash flow ratio. As things tighten up, banks can look to act — sometimes because your liquidity ratios are awry (i.e. too much debt for a given amount of assets, made worse by a drop in asset values).

Alternatively, debt servicing costs can rise or income can decrease, meaning your 'interest cover' is too thin. Remember the aspect of control. Avoid at all costs being put in a position of being forced to sell assets in a depressed or descending market. Act early to give yourself a buffer.

Warren Buffett's rules
Rule #1: Don't lose money. (Protect your capital.)
Rule #2: Remember rule #1.

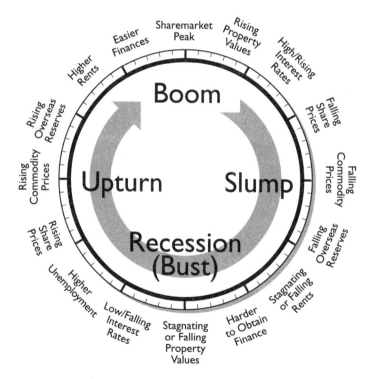

Figure 6.1   The economic clock (property clock)

How to survive and prosper in a falling property market

6

The Property Cycle

Mike McCombie and Peter Aranyi

Residential property is closely aligned to and affected by economic cycles (see previous chapter), and the residential market goes through its own property cycle. This is sometimes referred to as the *economic clock* or *property clock** where the high or boom is 12 o'clock, the slump is heading down from 3 o'clock to 6 o'clock (low, bust) and the recovery from 6 o'clock to 9 o'clock. The market 'moves' around the clock, sometimes forward — fast or slow — sometimes pausing, but moving on again after the pause. Essentially, it is moving constantly.

At different times in the cycle the market displays different characteristics. The boom phase, for example, is evidenced by an abundance of buyers. At this time there is lots of confidence, the world is full of optimists, and it is easy to obtain finance. However, in the slump phase market sentiment becomes overwhelmingly negative. It is much harder to raise finance and fewer people want to enter the market.

* The concept of the property cycle as a clock was popularised by London's *Evening Standard* newspaper early in the 20th Century. The face shows interlinking cyclical economic factors including interest rates, trade levels, ease of credit and real estate price growth. Property cycles were the topic of considerable attention through the 19th century, receiving their most convincing treatment by Henry George who summarized and developed earlier economists in his popular work *Progress and Poverty* (1879).

Characteristics of cycles

When trying to understand any cycle it can be useful to observe its characteristics. Factors to consider include:

- **Duration** – how long is the cycle generally, peak-to-peak or trough-to-trough, and how long are the various parts of the cycle, for example a typical *expansion* and *contraction* phase?

- **Stability** – does the cycle (and its various phases) tend to be volatile or fairly stable — and hence, to a certain extent, predictable?

- **Range and speed of change** – what has been the breadth of change — both up and down (e.g. does it double, or halve?) — and how quickly has the cycle moved from one stage to another in the past?

- **Drivers** – can you identify any influence affecting the progress of the market?

By reviewing these characteristics from past cycles you can get a feel for the current cycle, and sometimes extrapolate past events into the future. Your aim is to understand where a market might be in the current cycle and forecast when things might be changing — the point being to avoid surprise. This forecasting technique is certainly *not* exact but it can give us a feel for possible future scenarios.

What time is it?

So how do we know where we are in the property cycle — what time is it on the property clock? There are various economic indicators, some widely regarded as driving the housing market, which are recorded and published by government agencies like the Reserve Bank, Treasury and Statistics. Other measures are tracked by trading banks, investment brokers, large valuation firms, financial planners, and independent economic researchers. These factors are pored over endlessly by economists, politicians, boffins, the media and analysts of every sort. Some of these can give us clues. While this analysis is not foolproof — you won't find a 'magic bullet' or a completely accurate index (despite claims to the contrary) — together these records can help you build up a picture.

Predicting cycles

There's a lot of hogwash about predicting the residential property cycle propagated by various parties, some with vested interests. As Olly Newland colourfully points out, amateur economists, some acting as window dressing for property spruikers, can dazzle the gullible with complex models which seek to 'explain' the property cycle in pseudo-scientific terms. Naïve investors taking this self-promotion at face value can be confused … or worse, taken advantage of.

Professional, qualified economists — those representing the trading banks or large institutions (Westpac, NAB, AMP, ING etc) and university academics who study aspects of the market — produce higher quality information, in our experience. They may or may not be investors themselves, but their data and associated commentary is usually broader-based, better researched and *impartial* (i.e. not advocating a particular investment).

The value of proper, rigorous analysis sometimes lies not so much in directly 'forecasting' the housing market but in gathering and highlighting hard historical data — in exceptional cases, identifying new paradigms by drawing out long-term trends, demonstrating fundamental, even generational shifts in the market.

An excellent source of such analysis is Australian property economist Garrick R Small. Dr Small's research paper *Long Term Property Prices: Implications for Sydney Residential Development* presented to the International Cities, Town Centres & Communities Society conference in Sydney in 2008 and his earlier work *The Significance of Debt, Human Nature and the Nature of Land on Real Estate Cycles* presented to the Pacific Rim Real Estate Society 2000 International Conference, also in Sydney, contain valuable insights about the property market — drawn from years of study and incisive, detailed thought and statistical modelling.

This work is worth your attention. Key among Garrick Small's conclusions is the idea that the social-psychological aspects of property (market sentiment, herd behaviour and confidence) outweigh the more commonly discussed economic/pseudo-physics model.

What drives booms? Instead of fiddle-faddling around with short-term market-specific factors like vacancy rates, construction activity and the number of listings, (watching *suburbs*) as some do, Dr Small's analysis identifies long-term drivers, e.g. dwindling fertility and increased female participation in the work force since the 1960s — which saw a generational jump in family income. This step change affected housing affordability and drove a long rise (boom) in prices. The onset of that 'novel' second income enabled families to sustain debt at higher levels than previous generations.

As the effect of that income surge was absorbed (the second income became essential to the financial obligations of the household) in the early 1990s, along came another historical driver: the easy availability of cheap credit — accompanied by a societal change in attitude towards it, from 'debt is negative and we must get rid of it as quickly as possible' to 'debt is a sure and certain way to create wealth'. In a word: *confidence*.

The historic debt-fuelled housing boom resulted from (1) easy credit and (2) the revised social view of debt. As *The Day the Bubble Bursts* records, household borrowing ballooned

... and then exploded. Eventually, the market had to correct. Hence, the sub-prime crisis and global credit crunch.

We noted at the beginning of this book that a useful strategy for success is to seek a range of sources of neutral, *impartial* information, hard data and unbiased commentary about factors affecting your segment of the property market — from those with relevant experience. It can also be enlightening to consider the impact of social and psychological trends identified by researchers like Garrick Small.

You should discount the narrow one-sided analysis of property promoters or their 'hired gums'. (If they're selling, it's *always* time to buy.) Remember, the Real Estate Institute represents the interests of its members: real estate agents — and fair enough. Don't confuse such commentary with work whose conclusions result from dispassionate research and analysis.

Summary — residential market

As an investor, it can be useful to reflect on some of the micro- or macro-economic factors identified by the Reserve Bank and economists — as well as more down-to-earth measures identified by experienced investors (see next section). If it suits you, correlate for yourself their rise and fall in relation to your particular market or area of investment activity. This can help give you a feel for where that market sits in relation to the property clock. By all means, track such data relevant to your market — *then think for yourself.* Don't allow yourself to be spoon-fed homogenised, self-serving and ultimately very expensive market 'advice' by what is effectively part of a property sales operation.

As we noted in *Commercial Real Estate Investor's Guide*, while the economic factor/driver analysis discussed has some real value, *market sentiment* is the indicator we pay most attention to.

Commercial real estate cycles

Most of the time, the commercial property market does not correspond to the general economic cycle as closely as the residential property market. However the different types of commercial property are influenced to varying degrees by these economic and residential cycles.

Retail properties (shops, etc) tend to correspond most closely to the general economic cycle, followed by the warehousing and industrial sectors. The office sector is the least-aligned, in part due to the large cost of office buildings; before developers start building new office buildings, the fundamentals (rental levels, vacancy rates, building and finance costs etc) need to have shifted significantly in their favour before a development project in this sector makes sense. Instead of a seven to eight year economic cycle, the full office cycle is more like fifteen to eighteen years. However, all property sectors will be affected to some extent by the general economic cycles and, as mentioned, by market (and particularly *lender*) confidence.

There are also factors which will tell us where the commercial property market is in the cycle as well. Following is a chart that lists some of the determinants of value in relation to commercial property and how they react in boom or slump conditions. By reviewing current conditions and trends in these drivers you can get an idea of where the market is and, just as importantly, perhaps where it is going.

Commercial property value drivers

Value driver or indicator	12 o'clock (boom)	6 o'clock (slump or bust)
Market described as	'Strong'	'Weak'
Capitalisation rates	Low	High
Values	High	Low
Rentals	High	Low
Tenant demand	High	Low
Vacancy period	Short	Long
Tenant inducement needed	Low	High
Confidence	High	Low
Ease of bank lending	High	Low
Building costs	High	Low
Discount for vacancy	Low	High
Number of buyers	High	Low
Number of sellers	Low	High
No. of owner-occupiers	High	Low
Sentiment	Positive	Negative
Value of spare land and space	High	Low

Table 6.2   Value drivers in commercial property

Keep an eye on the value drivers

Regularly review the general market conditions and what you regard as the drivers determining value. Look at the list of value drivers for commercial property above and try to make a judgment about where they are in the cycle. They will all be affected and will move — the extent of the move depends on the severity of the fall in property values and the state of the economy.

The commercial property cycle 5–15 years

Bankers can't lend enough on commercial property – rumours of banking deals done on hand shakes at Airport lounges

Confidence/arrogance/long lunches pervasive

Top restaurants preferred lunch venue

Average age of property executives 25

Property yields at their lowest

Banks set up specialist property lending divisions

CBD tenants consider moving to suburbs

Vacancy rate below 4%

Stock brokers tip listed property companies as growth stocks

Marked increase in cranes on the skyline

Financing proposals all include steep rent growth projections

Net ratchetted BOMA (landlord-friendly) lease predominant

Developers declare quite substantial older buildings 'obsolete' — ripe for redevelopment

Several property development companies listed

Development schemes ubiquitous

Banks relax lending criteria

Land values double in one year as developers compete for sites

Valuers valuing properties 10% too low

Rent growth strong

Contributory mortgage companies emerge and high risk lenders providing mezzanine debt

Several schemes (development) in the market struggle to find tenants

Property yields fall significantly   Property yields peak

Property investment companies listed – sold as income stock

Property recovery commences via increase in sales volume

1 crane seen on skyline

Rents bottom out

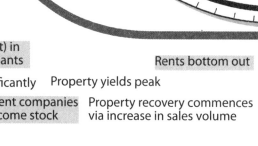

How to survive and prosper in a falling property market

Figure 6.3 This slightly world-weary version of the property clock was generated by commercial broker Tim Julian. It's a useful reminder that the market cycle *turns* — and that this is nothing new. Note how the commercial value drivers vary (and how 'denial of market weakness' is actually an indicator!)

Rents Peak   First lease incentives appear

Many cranes on skyline   Mortgagee sales become more prevalent

Property company shares fall sharply

Property leaders/experts deny the market is weak

Listed property developers are in liquidation

Contributory mortgage companies fall over

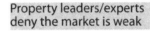

Gross unratchetted (tenant-friendly) leases prevail

Valuers valuing 10% too high

Property market acknowledges the market is weak

Banks refuse all proposals for vacant property

Rents in free fall

Leasing incentives peak

Change of use developments common

All cranes disappear from skyline

All but most conservative listed property companies in liquidation

Banks refuse all commercial property lending proposals

Fear is tangible in the property market – you can cut it with a knife

Own desk is preferred lunch venue

Vacancy rates peak

Debt to property yield gap widest (5%+)

Average age of property executive 45

Source: Tim Julian, Ray White Commercial Wellington

Some serious investors *look forward* to the next recession, because often that is where they've made their best deals in the past and made the most money. It is much harder finding good deals when the market is buoyant. It is fantastic being an investor *with the ability to buy* when Mr Market is depressed.

For the rest of this chapter, let's use the drivers above as categories to review some of the conditions that are likely to occur in a falling market and the subsequent challenges for the investor. The bigger the slump, the more accentuated the effects. (Also see Fig 6.3 *The commercial property cycle* pages 80-81.)

Capitalisation rates

Most commercial property is valued as follows:

Gross rental
Less non recoverable outgoings
= net rental
Divided by capitalisation rate
= Building value

The capitalisation rate (cap rate) is calculated as equal to the yields that a similar property with similar lease profile is selling for in the current market. Yield = net rental expressed as a percentage of the sale price of a property. For a more in-depth look at how capitalisation rates work refer to *Commercial Real Estate Investor's Guide* (see recommended reading).

Essentially, as the market booms, (1) rents climb and (2) cap rates move lower and lower. This has a doubly positive effect on building values, which is great for the commercial investor on the way up. Remember, as cap rates get lower, property values increase. (At the height of a boom you'll see headlines like: 'Commercial property yields at 15-year low' and predictions yields may drop even lower and into uncharted territory. This is typical of what you hear at the top end of a cycle. Remember the earlier comment that in our experience the market will always correct towards its trend line.)

As the market turns, buyers and tenants will retreat to varying degrees. Rents and yields shrink back, resulting in a fall in building values. The larger the correction, the greater the fall. It seems strange: your building and lease arrangements may be *exactly the same* as they were a few months earlier — same tenants, same lease profile — but now the investment is worth *less* simply because of this market-wide reduction in cap rates and market rents. If it is vacant, the impact of having it re-valued (for finance etc) in a lower market rent/higher cap rate environment could be dramatic.

The margin for risk varies with the market cycle

Another thing to be aware of is the *margin for risk*. Normally investors want a margin for risk, and demand a higher return to entice them to purchase riskier properties — i.e. lower grade, poorly located, or vacant properties. As the market slumps, the margin for risk required will increase. Valuers will apply a higher cap rate (lower value) to these less-than-prime and vacant buildings. At the top of the cycle with buyers vying to obtain property, there is often no margin, or a very low margin, allowed for this risk.

To help understand the impact of this, let's look at a (simplified) real example with dollar amounts.

Case study:
An industrial property near a main centre at the top of the market.
Net market rental $100,000
Net income, 6-year lease $100,000
Cap rate 7%
Value = $1,428,000

At the top of the market, that building could be put on the market *vacant* and it will probably still get the full $1,428,000 or close to it. In those circumstances, there is often no margin (or a very low differential) for vacancy or other risk i.e. the cap rate applied to calculate value would still be 7%. Often the selling agent will describe it as 'a great owner-occupier opportunity' — selling to all those would-be tenants who want this type of investment opportunity. (The world is full of optimists who are just happy to secure the purchase, and greedy not to miss out. Bless them.)

So in a strong market, the picture for that same property vacant could still be as follows or close to it:

> Market rental $100,000
> Net income   zero
> Cap rate (on market income)   7%
> **Value = $1,428,000**

However in a slump the scenario may be quite different. Imagine that rents dropped by 10%, and cap rates for fully-leased properties moved from 7% to 9% — a drop of 2% (remember, higher cap rate = lower value). We will also assume cap rates for vacant property jumped to 11% — that's realistic.

Let's look at the impact of that on the value of the building in dollar terms (that is, *your* dollars if you are the owner).

> Fully tenanted 6 year lease
> Market rent $90,000, (reflecting recent leasings and softer market)
> Net passing income $100,000
> (i.e. rent being received under current lease)
> Cap rate (applied to passing income) 9%
> **Value = $1,111,000**

Now let's see what would happen if you had to drop the rent to $90,000 to keep the existing tenant or secure a new one at market rent.

Fully tenanted 6 year lease
Market rent $90,000, (reflecting recent leasings and softer market)
Net passing income $90,000 (rent received under the new lease)
Cap rate on passing income 9%
Value = $1,000,000

Finally, let's look at the worst-case scenario in which you cannot attract a tenant and your property stays vacant at (or near) the low point in the cycle:

The same property *vacant* may only attract an 11% yield or cap rate. (In a severe correction and if the property was fringe or less-than-desirable, the cap rate applied could be a lot higher than 11% resulting in a further decrease in value.)

Market rental $90,000
Income zero (vacant)
Cap rate applied to potential market rent 11%
Value = $818,000

This is a drop in value of $610,000 (nearly 43%) from its value at the top of the cycle!

If you're looking for a great way to lose money, or destroy wealth (even faster than divorce) this is it: Buy a fully tenanted property, pay full value at the top of a cycle (or worse, pay *over market* because of fear of missing out) and then find yourself forced to sell it — vacant — at the bottom in a slump!

Now imagine if you were 80% geared on the up-front valuation of $1,428,000. Your debt would be $1,142,000. You could be in all sorts of strife (to put it politely) if you were forced to sell, getting the then full market price of only $818,000, rather than being able to ride the slump out.

It happens, and it will happen again.

Trust me; it is much more fun being the purchaser than the seller in these circumstances.

Values and value of the spare bits

Generally values will drop in a slump. Buyers and tenants will go to ground to varying degrees — withdrawing from the market in fright. Something that happens as a result is that the value of those extra bits (like untenanted building space, extra land, car parks etc) is discounted strongly.

At the top of the market buyers have to pay for anything extra with very low margins for risk or leasing up. There might be some 'spare' land with the site, but you have to pay full land value. As discussed, in a boom, vacant buildings are often sold for the same values as if they were fully leased.

When the market slumps, any 'extra bits' are very heavily discounted (sometimes totally). In a slump, buildings are often sold at a price based solely on their passing rental with little or no value allocated to the spare bits. What an opportunity!

Rentals

There will be pressure on rentals to fall back. Some landlords will be under pressure and the negotiating power definitely shifts over to the tenants. At the top of the cycle landlords have the luxury of tenants competing to lease property, but after a significant correction of the cycle there may be few (if any) potential tenants. Tenants in the market will know this, and if you are a landlord you may have to offer all sorts of *inducements* to entice them into your space (or to keep them in) — things like rent holidays, a contribution to their fitout, reduced rent and management fees, or caps on outgoings.

If you or other landlords agree to lower rentals (as some will be forced to do) then the valuers' assessments of market rentals will also be reduced. They will use this latest evidence to establish current rentals, and this will directly impact on your building's value.

Tenants and tenant demand

There will be fewer tenants and you will have to work harder and offer more to attract them and to keep them. Remember, as commercial leases come up for renewal, the tenants will be free to shop around. There will be other landlords aggressively working to secure any tenants they can get to fill their vacant property.

As a landlord, you need to manage this risk. Look after your tenants well and work to secure them early at renewal. (If you can, whenever you sign up a new lease, try to put a long notice period for renewal.) If you need to offer them something to stay, see if you can come up with incentives while protecting the passing rent or the nominal rent which a valuer will value your property on. Consider making a lump sum contribution to their fitout or upgrade, or a rent holiday, even a loan, in favour of offering a rent reduction.

Some tenants will come under pressure

In commercial property some businesses, especially retail, will be under pressure at the bottom end of the cycle — their profits will be squeezed, some will be barely surviving. Some of your commercial tenants will leave, some will default, and some will collapse. Some will want to leave (default on their lease), or to downsize or shut down. This sort of tenant behaviour will increase as pressure rises. Be prepared for it.

It is therefore important to closely look at your tenants (or prospective tenants) when you are preparing leases. Check out how their business is doing. Always demand personal guarantees, and review their statements of position and credit ratings. Alternatively, seek bank guarantees on your leases — this is much more common with commercial leases these days. When you are buying a property, thoroughly research the tenants to establish the health of their business, their whole business sector, and how strong they might be at the downside of the cycle.

Residential tenants are also going to be under more pressure. High employment levels may soften a downturn but if the economy changes substantially for the worse then there will inevitably be some staff laid off, or their work hours reduced, or made redundant when the factory is shifted overseas. Some will go bankrupt, some won't pay their rent on time, others will string you along as long as possible.

The landlord as banker!

When times get tough, tenants don't pay rent on time, they miss payments, and will use you as the bank if they can. Residential and commercial tenants may want to use you, the landlord, as a source of cheap credit. Other creditors will try this as well. This may impact on your cash flow. (Of course, this usually happens when you're already stretched and have decreased resources.) Keep on top of your cash flow — tightly monitor your payments in and out. Have good systems established so that you can keep track of your income accurately and efficiently.

While times are good, establish a buffer or emergency fund to see you through the leaner times. You'll sleep better and sweat the small stuff a lot less.

Keep your standards

If you are a residential landlord it is crucial to choose your tenants carefully — check their credit and their references, keep your residential rental management tight and up-to-date. This is critical, especially when times are hard. If you let things get behind and do not collect the rent on time etc, then when the outstanding amount gets too large, you'll often find it hard to recover the lost rent.

Don't make the mistake of compromising your standards to get an undesirable tenant — you are better to carry the vacancy a little longer and search for a reliable and trustworthy tenant. Again, you can only afford to do this if you have not pushed yourself to the limits. Make sure you have a buffer of rents over servicing costs, allowing for some vacancies, so that you can afford to carry some vacancy.

In my earlier days as a residential landlord I put tenants into a flat because I was a bit desperate for the cash flow, I also made the situation worse by not managing my tenants closely at the time, I was too focused on doing more deals and not focused enough on tightly managing the properties I had.

As a result I suffered significant losses when the tenants vandalised the property, literally smashing every wall and fitting in the house. Then they left without paying the rent. Never again. I would rather leave a house vacant for a little longer until I found the right tenant. This experience encouraged me to manage my properties more carefully. (This was a useful lesson, but one that really hurt at the time.)

Landlord and tenant relationships

In a downturn, there can be increased tension between landlords and tenants when things get difficult. Commercial tenants can threaten to leave at lease renewal unless you give them inducements to stay such as improved fitout or a rent reduction. (And remember, in a tight market other landlords really want tenants! If *you* had a vacant building, it is likely you would be prepared to offer inducements to fill it. So would they. That is just how the market operates.) In short, look after your tenants, and don't play hardball with them. Cash flow is critical at this stage. Without it you are exposed. Take the time to ask yourself: What's the downside of being tough with my tenant and saying: "Sorry, that's the market rent"? What situation am I going to be in if the tenant leaves and my building is vacant? (Remember, with commercial space, your building's value is tightly bound to what it is rented for.)

Look for a trade-off: If you give them something, see if you can tie them into the lease for longer. This sort of arrangement will help you survive a hard period and give you some security — and a slightly improved cap rate.

Be prepared for longer vacancies

Sometimes, despite your best efforts, you just cannot attract a tenant. (This is especially relevant for commercial properties: generally, with a residential investment, if you keep dropping the rent, you'll find a tenant.)

Be wary of buying vacant property, especially fringe property such as low-grade office space in areas not in high demand; or low stud warehouses with columns i.e. not clear span, or in secondary locations; or retail with low pedestrian counts and poor exposure. Avoid these unless your other cash flow is strong and your debt is low. A property may seem cheap — especially compared to what buyers were paying for it at the top of the cycle — but if you can't get a tenant and you are then forced to sell it vacant as well (rather than ride it out) you may find its value has dropped even further.

Management systems

Sadly, employees and others working for you can also come under financial pressure and it is important to ensure that your financial and management systems are tight enough to track all payments and ensure they are going where they are meant to and not off to the side to financially support an errant staff member.

One of the best things about property investment is the freedom it gives you. When investors do really well they often want to skive off and enjoy their lifestyle.

Remember it is your business and your money — and hence ultimately your responsibility to look after it. Before you leave your investments in the hands of others, check your systems. e.g. who signs the cheques and sets up the automatic payments? If not you, then make sure you have sound systems in place to protect you. Even if you regard the monitoring and signing cheques as mildly inconvenient, it will not be nearly as inconvenient as realizing that for the last six months or more payments have not been going where they should and finding you are seriously out of pocket. It happens. Be warned.

Confidence

At the top of the cycle the world is full of optimistic 'experts'. Through a boom, property investing is flavour of the month. People love it. Even tenants will be saying, "Let's become owner-occupiers and own our premises rather than paying rent."

Lots of residential investors and newcomers have come into the commercial market, looked at the historically *low* commercial returns and said, "Wow aren't these fantastic returns compared to residential?" Generally speaking, the people making these statements simply do not understand the historical context.

The main emotion in a booming market is greed. If there is any fear, it is the fear of missing out — scarcity, which drives prices even higher.

At times like this, banks and funders love commercial property, and people are comfortable taking a punt on vacant property. Even second-grade, marginal property sells at prime property yields. "You can't lose!" the agents say.

Oh, really?

Sorry, but we've seen this before. As with any cycle, the environment will change.

The further we go into a slump (and the stronger or deeper the slump) the more confidence evaporates. The driving emotion moves from greed to fear. Fear of loss. Fear of doing anything. 'Analysis-paralysis'.

Property values drop and the former tenants, now owner-occupiers, will now be saying, "What were we thinking? There's no money in this game." Many will be under pressure in their own business and to help retire debt or just obtain some cash they will sell at the bottom of the market. Their aim now is to retrench, to return to what they know. If you are set up and ready to move you can assist them with this strategy. This can be a great investment opportunity

In a slump, people will have been burnt. More and more will shun property investment and disparage it. They will increasingly be risk-averse and looking to protect themselves.

Bouncing back from a setback

If you have been burnt, have lost money or been caught in the contraction, this can be a very challenging time. Do you give up property investment and do something else? That might be *exactly* what all your loved ones are urging you to do. Or do you take the lessons you have been handed and start again?

I came out of bankruptcy in 1993 and I remember in 1994 telling my wife that I had found a 'great deal'. I told her I could fund it without cash and that it would get us started again. I had done all my calculations *really carefully* and the deal stacked up — it 'worked' on paper. But boy, was I scared! Extremely fearful. Had I made a mistake? Were my numbers correct? What if I got it wrong again? And my wife was feeling the same. Sadly, but understandably, her trust in me was very low. Both of us were scarred from my past mistakes and how hard I had pushed it.

Together we reviewed the numbers and all of my assumptions. We talked it through, went for a walk, allowed ourselves some space and came back to it again. It was pretty edgy stuff and very challenging on our relationship. I still have enormous respect for my wife who eventually said she trusted me and agreed to us going for the deal.

It wasn't the last time I stretched her as I worked my way back with larger and larger deals again, but it was one of the hardest.

Where have all the buyers gone?

In the slump, property investment is no longer flavour of the month — and many buyers will retreat and go to ground. Any urgency in the market will dissipate and agents will have to work hard to attract buyers. Many 'buyers' will be tyre-kickers, just looking. Most will be very cautious and only want to buy real bargains or steals.

Many of those owner-occupiers (who thought it was crazy to rent when they could own) become sellers. Tenants also have more negotiating power and can negotiate significantly improved rental deals.

Add all this to the fact that there are more sellers generally and it is fairly easy to see why yields increase, values come back and sale prices drop.

That completes my summary of the drivers identified in table 6.2.

Let's move on to discussing what can be a real 'crunch factor' — a make-or-break issue for those in the property game throughout the cycle: funding.

7

The changing face of your lender

Mike McCombie

I'm happy to say I have an excellent relationship with my funders.* It hasn't always been that way, but these days it's great. I remember someone saying, for your own financial safety you should regard lenders as 'fair-weather friends' and always take steps to protect yourself from their clutches when the worm turns. This may sound harsh, even cynical — but it is worth being aware of how things work and why some investors might reach those conclusions.

In a rising market, with banks aggressively competing for lending business they will often relax their lending criteria — offering high loan-to-value ratios, looser interest cover requirements, easy interest-only terms, and large general unsecured overdrafts. In a buoyant market, lenders are much more forgiving of, for instance, missed payments or bounced automatic payments, and will ignore some issues. However, when the market softens and falls, all that changes.

* Throughout this chapter I will use the words 'bank', 'lender' and 'funder' interchangeably.

The very same institutions will tighten up. Suddenly they want to have security for everything. Your 'normal' mortgage reviews suddenly become more than a formality. New property and rental valuations can be ordered. (Remember our case study of dropping value — watch out!) All the fine print on your credit agreements now means something. Your unused revolving finance or line of credit can be changed in a heartbeat, even cancelled. Bank managers who may have had a great deal of discretion and independent lending approval ability can suddenly find their lending limits chopped. It only takes a few loans to go bad (default) for head office to withdraw privileges and demand results from bank managers.

In a slump, *everything* tightens up and this will have an affect on your ability to get credit. It's ironic: in a booming market it is easy to get loans but harder to find bargains because you face lots of competition, then, in a slump, it is easier to find the bargains but harder to *fund* them because the lenders are wary. Some are running scared. (Just another of life's challenges.) Notably, it can also be an opportunity, because it means there are fewer other investors set up and actually able to buy property.

Interest rates

Mortgage interest is often the investor's biggest expense. Changes in interest rates affect people in all sectors of the economy. Worldwide, we've had a period of interest rates sitting at low levels not seen for 40 years. They have risen from these lows (what else could they do?)

Many property owners and investors have been cushioned from the effects of earlier rate rises because of fixed interest loans — where their mortgages have been fixed at low rates. Increasingly, these loans will come up for refinancing at higher rates. This will put pressure on some owners whose cash flow is already tight. Some will be forced to sell. (Make sure this does not affect you! Or if it does affect you, sell sooner while the market is still strong, rather than selling when you are really stretched and in a depressed market.) The higher interest rates go, the more pressure there will be. Rolling over a mortgage from 6% to 9% is a 50% increase in mortgage funding costs. (If an investment was barely cash flow positive with lending at 6% interest rate in place, at 9% it's going to be going backwards fast and will probably need to be supported from other cash flow.)

Just imagine if interest rates went to 15%. This has happened before.

This mortgage-funding crunch will put pressure on some people who pushed everything to the limit with cash flow at break-even or less.

Think of all those properties that have been purchased at 7% yields — or even lower, down to 5%. Interest rates have already risen to 10% or more which means that even with 50% gearing you are only virtually break-even on the purchase price.

In a slump, where interest rates rise, there will be owners who are simply too highly geared and who will be forced to sell because of cash flow pressure.

Lenders are likely to tighten their criteria

The lenders' cost of funds will be higher — so they in turn will use higher borrowers' rates when assessing the affordability of your proposed deals. Imagine, for example, that the floating rate is 9%, they may want you to use 10% or 10.5% for your budget calculations — to show how your deal will look if interest rates rise some more.

Lenders usually want income-to-interest cover of one-and-a-half times, or they want servicing costs to be no more than

30% to 35% of income from the property. Because there is limited scope to increase income or rents (in fact there can be pressure just to hold rents in a slump), these constraints on debt servicing can lead lenders to require lower levels of borrowing on a building purchase. They will look at your loan-to-value ratios (LVR), and they will start to tighten up sharply. This is demonstrated in their (un)willingness to entertain 'non-conforming' loans. Basically, they become much less flexible.

As I've mentioned above, banks lend to a percentage of the value of a property (LVR). A lot of house loans are calculated on 80% or 90% of valuation. These ratios can (and do) change throughout the cycle with the banks' enthusiasm to fund property. As prices drop, valuers will follow with lower valuations, and if the banks start to feel 'exposed' they will require updated valuations — which naturally will be lower. If the banks combine this lower valuation with a reduction in their LVRs then there is a double hit against investors. The property has a lower value and the banks will only lend to a lower percentage of this lower value.

Hence, lenders will require either additional security or demand debt reduction (a lump of cash).

Some owners will not be in a position to meet this — their borrowing capacity will have been reached already (they're 'maxed out'.) So they will be pressured to sell at the bottom of the market — which is the one thing you want to avoid. (Remember Mr Market: you must *choose* when you sell your property. The aim is to buy property at the bottom of the market, not sell it then!)

Also, as interest rates increase, your cash flow (and your ability to borrow) *decreases*. This is another fact of life.

Beware the bank's changing 'favourites'

If the banks no longer 'like' a particular segment of the market (e.g. residential investment properties or vacant commercial or bare development land) they are likely to dial back the percentage of what they will lend on valuation. For example, a while ago the banks decided they'd lent enough on inner-city apartments especially in Auckland. They believed there would be a fall in apartment values. They had lent in the past to 80% even 90% of valuation, but almost overnight reduced this to 65% or 70%. As a result, many investors and buyers could no longer fund apartment purchases they had committed to. So some intending purchasers just could not proceed. Therefore the values fell — just as the banks had anticipated! (What part did they play in accentuating the fall in value with their lending policy changes?) Be careful when the bank is no longer excited by, or welcoming, the type of property investment you are investing in. Consult with them in advance and keep checking.

Diverging interests

Banks and lenders will always protect their own interests first — this is fair enough if you are a lender! Usually when you apply to borrow bank money, the bank has money to lend and wants to do so, as that is their business. So you have the same interests. But there are times when those interests diverge — your interests and the lender's go in opposite directions.

As values and market confidence fall, this is where the bank's and the investor's interests diverge the most. For example, when the bank really loses confidence in your ability to repay your loan to them, they may (or will) initiate a mortgagee sale of your property. Before they get to that stage, they will formally tell you to resolve your arrears and bring your accounts up to date etc. They'll explicitly warn you: "If you do not get this loan in order, we will sell you up — foreclose on the loan."

Essentially, lenders want to clear the debt and receive the interest due. You need to understand that lenders will seek to do so even if that means selling up at the expense of you the owner. Mortgagee sales — and bank-directed forced sales to head off a mortgagee sale — multiply during the down part of the cycle.

There can be a great opportunity here as you can often get a property for the bank debt plus some of interest — in other words, a price that relates far less to its value and more to the debt owed. (This is most unfortunate if you are the seller.)

You may also have a lender approaching you at the bottom of the market saying, 'We want you to repay your loan.' It is really important to maintain a good relationship with your lenders. You do not want to become one of those people with whom the bank is getting tough. We will cover this in more detail in the next chapter, *Funding tips*, but a good primary defensive strategy is to spread your loans between lenders. This reduces your exposure to any one bank or lender and gives you more flexibility to juggle finance if necessary.

When a lender feels over-exposed

Things change. Sometimes the bank's head office (which these days is often in another country, for New Zealand, read Australia) decides that they have enough exposure — or worse, *too much* exposure — to the property sector, or a segment of it. Firstly they will just stop lending to that sector — or they will price the margin for lending (interest rate) at a premium to discourage more lending.

When they *want* the business they may agree to lend you the money at 1%–1.5% above the bank bill rate, but when they're not keen, they'll raise this margin to 2.5% or more.

Worse, you'll hear about banks just 'switching off' lending to, say inner-city apartments or spec homes, construction projects or vacant commercial property. It means they are feeling uncomfortable about their exposure, and just don't want any more.

When banks take the next step and decide they are *overexposed* (i.e. have too much lending) to a particular sector — they will actively take steps to reduce that exposure. Lenders will focus first on marginal and badly-managed or 'non-performing' client loans and try to get them repaid, or get the LVRs improved (i.e. debt lowered). However, as happened after 1987, when they could not reduce their exposure enough by targeting these 'distressed' clients, they'll then go after well-behaved clients with sound loans and good repayment histories. They pressure these 'good' clients to get *them* to reduce their debt — either by repaying lump sums of cash or bringing in additional security, or worse, by selling up to clear the bank's debt. This can be very stressful if you're the borrower.

So although you may have a really good relationship with your bank or lender, usually with the bank manager you deal with, if the bank *stops lending altogether* (it happens, believe me) you just cannot get money from them. The directive has come from higher up the food chain and you may not have a relationship with those managers who are just doing it by the numbers. If the bank's head office puts these changes through, all managers underneath have to follow it.

A true story: A bank mortgage manager got an email from head office telling him to reduce the bank's exposure to 'property investors'. Being a good bureaucrat, and looking to make a good start, he called his 'best' client and told him the bank wasn't happy with the loan-to-value ratio over his portfolio of about twenty residential rental properties — all funded with the same bank and with cross-collateral security (mortgages spread over the whole lot). "We need you to reduce your debt level, John," he said. "You need to kick in about $200,000."

"But Bill, I don't have $200,000," the investor spluttered. "You were happy enough to lend me money a few months ago."

"Sorry, John," the mortgage manager said, "if you haven't got the money, that's not my problem, that's your problem." And under pressure from the bank, the investor launched a fire-sale. "He lost the lot," the mortgage manager told us a few years later. That's how they treat their 'best' customers?! This is not an isolated case.

Another investor had a call from a bank saying, "Our valuers say your commercial building would have dropped in value so your lending ratio's all wrong. We need a lump sum mortgage reduction of $160,000 from you by next week."

"I don't have it," was the investor's reply.

"In that case, we'll sell you up!" said the banker.

A defensive strategy you need to adopt *before* you need it is to develop and maintain funding relationships with several banks and lenders, and to also build good relationships with finance brokers. Brokers are often the ones who know where the best finance deals are and which lenders are still lending on your type of project or property sector. Keep working on the funding side. Don't let this part of your investment strategy slide, because as we've already said, as the market falls, funding gets harder — for everyone. At the bottom of the cycle, you can get a bank coming to you out of the blue — whether at a scheduled review or not — and demanding that you repay or partially repay a loan as the examples above demonstrate. Prepare for it. This doesn't usually happen during a minor correction, unless your ratios are on the edge but is a very real possibility in a major slump.

Changes in decision-making

When the market is buoyant and property vales are rising, lenders share everyone else's excitement and confident assurance that 'the only way is up'. They feel less at risk and as a result can be fairly lenient with lending criteria. But as the market tightens, that changes. During the early part of a slump, you'll find the banks will become increasingly gun-shy — this is evident in an increase in the time it takes them to make lending decisions and process the deals. They appear almost reluctant to lend, nervously taking much longer to consider your finance proposal and requiring more information and full disclosure of your affairs.

The lender's head office wants every bit of information and every box ticked before their approval will come through. They will sometimes want to examine company accounts and financial statements because as the slump deepens they will have found out they've been duped by some of their other clients — borrowers who failed to disclose negative things which came out of the closet later. The bank's trust level towards its clients (even you) will be much lower. The lending team will be more cynical and defensive.

So if you sign up a conditional deal, be careful to *allow for* this extra decision-making time by your lender. Don't make the conditional period too tight. Or if you go unconditional with a deadline for settlement, and you know you'll have to do a bit of juggling, do not waste time. Make sure you get your funding application to the lender early enough.

Some managers and banks will be burnt by bad loans in the slump. As a result, they will not make decisions quickly — sometimes they will not make them at all. The managers you have been working with will lose a lot of their discretion and decision-making ability as things tighten up. Managers will be transferred. (After the crash in 1987 one of my managers was 'promoted' to a branch where his branch overdraft limit was less than my own unsecured overdraft had been.) 'Bulldog' type replacement managers will be sent in to clean up 'problem' clients. This is not a pleasant experience for anyone.

Banks under pressure also display a much lower tolerance for problems with your account such as missed interest payments, delays in agreed lump-sum re-payments, etc.

They'll also act to 'resolve issues' to 'bring the account back into order' faster, with much less discretion and leeway. They'll run a tighter ship and offer you much less support. They're looking over their shoulder to see how their actions will be perceived by their manager. (Remember the bureaucrat's overriding value: *safety from criticism*. CYA: Cover your arse.)

Second-tier lenders under pressure

In a slump, second-tier funders, mezzanine funders and finance companies will also be under much more pressure. These lenders can be crucial for developers and smaller commercial property investors. They routinely lend to a higher percentage of valuation — usually on top of or 'behind' bank funding. They also lend to people and businesses on the edge (sometimes they're the last resort, and why else would people pay their higher rates?) They also tend to lend to developers who are often greatly exposed in a falling market.

In a slump, these lenders will have more of their loan book (their portfolio of loans) turn sour. Borrowers go into default as the cowboys are exposed. The lenders will call in any additional security quickly, and take the other steps they have established to protect themselves. Their margins for risk will increase — making this 'higher risk' money even *more* expensive — just when you might need it!

8

Funding tips

Mike McCombie

Spread your business

As I've already emphasised, do *not* place all your business with one bank or lender. If all your lending is with one funder they will likely have a mortgage over all your assets and they will also want guarantees for everything. As we've seen, banks can change their appetite for a particular type of property overnight and even — usually temporarily — just not want to lend any more (or they will only do so if you agree to pay a higher interest rate or excessive fees). If all your assets are tied up with one bank and they say 'No', how do you get another funder interested?

So do not put all your eggs in one basket. Spread your lending around — this will mean resisting all the incentives offered, even demands, by your bank that they want 'all your business'. Resist. (Generally they'll offer you fee-free accounts, a discount margin on the interest rate, rebates on your insurance and lots of other goodies like airpoints, flybuys etc to try to get your business.) These discounts and incentives are simply not worth what they can do to you when things get tough.

Also, try to keep your family home out of the mix. Have a separate lender and, if possible, a separate legal entity for that asset. If possible, avoid cross-collateral security where the lender secures their loan over more than one property. If you have to agree to this to get the loan, insist on limiting it (i.e. specify which properties are offered as security, and get their agreement to review this arrangement once your equity in the new property covers the loan amount.) Always think carefully about what you're offering as security on any single deal. Don't give them more than you need to get the loan. Also, avoid needlessly agreeing to an excessive priority amount on a mortgage (the amount the lender secures over your property in exchange making a loan — they put a higher amount than the funds advanced, allowing for penalty interest and charges in the case of default). Leave room for extra borrowing from elsewhere. Be intelligent about these things when the market is strong so they don't put unnecessary pressure on you when it's weak.

Sinking fund

Use a sinking fund if you need to support cash flow. Establish an account that you can draw down as you need funds to pay expenses. It sounds counter-intuitive to have money on deposit in an account when you're borrowing, but it can be very comforting for the bank to see how you're managing, say, the development expenses.

Sometimes you can be short on cash flow but still have good equity. The sinking fund allows you to take advantage of this and relieve some short term pressure.

Be careful not to go on too long in this way, otherwise you can chew up all your equity.

Brokers

Sometimes it can be useful to use a finance broker to raise your finance rather than dealing directly with the bank or lender. Brokers often have access to funding sources you may not even be aware of. As mentioned, a good broker will also be informed about which lenders are currently the most competitive — or which lenders are still lending on your type of deal. Work to build relationships with more than one broker if you can, and ask other investors who they use and who they recommend. However, avoid shopping around too much or playing one broker off against others. Often the broker will be using some of the same sources of finance. As soon as your proposal for finance reaches the potential funder, they run a credit check on you. That credit check shows up on your records when the next one is carried out. Therefore, it quickly becomes apparent to funders that you are shopping around — or perhaps that you have been turned down by others. A possible solution to this is to request your own credit report from the credit reporting agency and give the funder a copy of it, telling them they can get it updated as a final condition of the advance. (Again, this retains your element of control.)

Ask for vendor finance

When buying, check out the possibility of vendor finance. This type of funding is much more common in a soft market. Ask the question. 'If you don't ask, the answer's always no'. If the vendor is willing, get them to leave in a *second* mortgage. If they want to limit the size of the first mortgage, try to get them to limit it to a *percentage* of the valuation rather than a dollar amount. That way as the value grows later, you can increase the size of the first mortgage, assuming the wording in your loan document allows this. Discuss with your lawyer how to achieve this.

Buy more slowly

Delay settlement or have a longer conditional period. When the market is slower, buy time. Set up your sale and purchase agreements with longer settlement and a longer conditional period, to give you time to work on things (funding being just one of them) without you facing holding costs or being under pressure. You can often get beneficial terms because there are fewer buyers competing with you. Don't needlessly put yourself into a pressure situation where you have to settle quickly — and therefore have to raise finance wherever and on whatever terms you can get.

Playing hardball

Don't play hardball with your lender when you are in strife, unless you really do have something that they want — e.g. some cash, property with equity or other assets — otherwise you are in a weak negotiating position.

A developer we know made the mistake of trying to be tough with his bank when he was in financial strife... and they already had him over a barrel.

In those days, the late 1980s, the banks would lend with just a mortgage on the property, and personal guarantee if they could get it. When things went wrong with the loan they would take action from this security — either force a sale or move to mortgagee auction or start bankruptcy proceedings.

In this case, the bank didn't already have a debenture security over the developer's property-owning company and when things started to look very bad, they wanted the developer to sign such a debenture in their favour. A debenture would have allowed them to appoint receivers and more easily get access to any of the other assets of the company, even if they were only tax losses. In short, it would allow the bank to act more quickly and globally.

So the bank manager said, "You owe us all this money and you cannot pay it back. Please sign here, giving us a debenture on the development company's assets."

Our developer friend mistakenly thought he was actually holding some cards and said he would sign *only* if the bank waived his personal guarantee. In reality, the bank didn't need the debenture to act. They were just shoring up their position. They took offence and decided that if he wasn't going to cooperate, they would begin bankruptcy proceedings.

The lesson: Do *not* play hardball with the bank in that sort of financial situation. Co-operate with them.

Debentures and GSAs

When banks lend to developers or professional investors they routinely ask for a General Security Agreement (GSA), which is essentially a debenture over the borrower's company (or asset-owning entity). This allows the lender to act more easily in the event of a default. You do not have to give them this however (remember, everything is negotiable) and one strategy is to say no.

They might not like it, but you can offer to sign a negative pledge — promising that you will not give any other party a GSA either. In our experience, this seems to make them slightly happier, i.e. they know that no other funder will get the security that they cannot have, so they relax a little. This saves you from having to implement a list of 'ranked' GSAs (first ranked, second ranked etc) over the ownership entity, which can become messy.

A lot of investors aren't aware you can also negotiate limitations to personal or trust guarantees, i.e. you can specifically exclude assets like 'the family home at 123 City Street and the Bach at 45 Beach St' from the guarantee — assuming you have enough assets to give the bank peace of mind that their position is covered.

Interest-only or principal-and-interest?

Many commercial or more substantial residential investors tend to favour interest-only loans, primarily because they don't like to tie up cash flow in principal reduction which is paid out of after-tax income. Paying off the principal is after-tax money whereas the capital growth is not taxable, as long as you are an investor, rather than a trader. If you're an investor wanting to make your money work for you as hard as possible and wanting to acquire as much property as you can, you'll favour interest-only loans.

Conventionally, banks will want you to agree to a principal-and-interest mortgage, and you can negotiate an interest-only loan for a couple of years with the understanding that at the end of that term you will change to a principal-and-interest arrangement — but hopefully you can re-negotiate at that stage to continue with interest-only.

Some banks and non-bank lenders offer longer term (10 year) interest-only loans, but most trading banks have a requirement for commercial loans that they like to see the debt down to about 40%–60% of the value of the property when your current lease expires. Therefore it is very important, especially in a slump, to work on lease renewals so that you approach your funder to renegotiate funding with a *tenanted* property rather than one becoming vacant. If you do not have a tenanted property at this re-negotiation stage, your lender can get anxious.

As we've discussed, the willingness and flexibility of lenders varies with the cycle. In a slump, they can be intransigent, stuck on their demands (e.g. that you take out a principal-and-interest table mortgage over a short term, say ten years, or that they'll only lend to a 50% loan-to-value ratio). A few short years later, given looser instructions from head office these very same bankers will almost twist your arm to borrow more money from them: "Interest-only? No problem. We can even go to 70%." Understand this: they are *not* cynically trying to ensnare you. It is just that the lending criteria change with the cycle, sometimes rapidly, and the lending officers operate under different incentives for different activities at different times of the cycle (just as you do).

Fixed interest

Should you use fixed-interest loans? It's up to you. Establish where you think interest rates are heading. Fixing an interest rate costs you some flexibility if you want to sell or refinance, but if these aren't likely issues for you, fixing your interest rate for four or five years can give you some cash flow certainty and protect you from interest rate increases. Some advisors suggest a diversification approach known as *interest rate averaging* — where you spread your fixed term loans over different periods so your loans do not all come up for review at the same time.

Using vendor funding and riding the cycle up

When the market is flat, down at the bottom, that is the time to negotiate 'non-price' items.

I bought property in Auckland, for example, in 2001 for $9 million. It consisted of 55 apartments plus five shops and had been on the market for six months without selling. I paid $7 million for the building and $2 million for a section of land next door. At that stage, the building was probably only worth $6 million to $6.5 million.

The owner was what we would politely call a 'prudent investor' (so tight that he squeaks when he walks) and he wouldn't budge on his price of $7 million. After much futile negotiating, we discussed him leaving some money in if I paid his asking price of $7 million. He agreed to leave in $5.85 million at 8% interest.

He wanted $2 million for the land. It was only worth $1.5 million at best, but again, he wouldn't budge on the price. I wanted car parking for the apartments; he agreed to leave in $2 million *interest free* for four years. This was a bonus for me because I knew I would struggle to fund this through the banks.

I delayed settlement on the apartments for six months, but our agreement gave me access to renovate. In that time I unit-titled the property and at the end of that process the valuation had increased to $11 million. (The difference in the valuation related to how it was valued as a block versus how it was valued as 55 individual titles.) So fairly soon I had funded it with 100% finance on my purchase price. (I borrowed the balance of the purchase price from a second-tier lender on a second mortgage).

It can be pretty difficult (and sometimes impossible) to get this sort of flexibility in a deal at the top of the market. In this case, the owner was happy because he had got his price. I was happy because the market was rising fast. In two-and-a-half years I sold that land next door for $4 million (this was before I had to settle the interest-free loan to buy it!) My buyer then sold it for $6 million (isn't a rising market wonderful?) As I write this, that owner is still trying to get a development to work based on that land value. This 'pass the parcel' stuff is typical of boom-time behaviour.

I also quietly sold down the apartments over the next few years for about $17 million, so ultimately this was a great deal for me. I was able to get this good deal by paying *more* than the property was worth but by negotiating on non-price items (possession and vendor finance) which bought me time to add value and take advantage of a rising market.

9

What can go wrong?

Mike McCombie

Let's look at some of the other factors that can rear up and bite you in a sliding or slumped market and some of the strategies you can follow to protect yourself as an investor and as a landlord. Remember, the more intense the slump, the more intense will be the negative pressures.

Buyers will walk (and not for the exercise!)

When the market is falling, buyers will walk away from deals where they've paid no deposits, or a small deposit, sometimes even when they have paid a large one.

Buyers will sometimes walk away from small deposits. You may think you've *sold* a property, at a good price but with a long-term settlement. If the market value drops 10% to 20% or more (as it certainly can in a large correction) then it may actually make more sense for your buyer to walk away and forfeit their deposit — even a 10% deposit — rather than compete the deal.

Yes, you can sue the buyer for specific performance for having defaulted on the contract — but if they have gone under (or are not worth anything) you have to look at the merits of this action. Legal proceedings are always negative, hugely time-consuming and expensive. Sometimes it is better to just carry on with more positive things.

The deposit and the agent

There are many traps for the vendor, and here's one of them: Often an agent will sell the property for you, and the deposit paid by the buyer is lodged into the agents' Trust account — the agent essentially only wants to have a deposit that covers their commission and fee (that's their need). Once you have a contract for sale and purchase, the agent is held to have done their job and they are paid. The deposit is released to them for their commission immediately — so if the deal falls over later and the deposit was small and only covers the agent's fees, you can get nothing! I normally structure the agent's commission so that if the deposit is small they get paid *on settlement*.

Let me say it again: In a flat or falling market, when only a small deposit is paid and things start getting harder, there is a real risk that your buyer will seek to escape from the agreement — simply walk away. Protect yourself from that eventuality and its negative repercussions. When you are negotiating a property sale, you have to cope with that familiar tension between (1) accepting any deal you can get — say with a low deposit and long settlement which means you are taking a risk around the deposit, and (2) holding out for a better deal and possibly losing the one on the table.

If you decide to accept a deal with a long settlement it's often useful to include a 'cash out' clause. (See Tony Steindle's section for an example.) This enables you to give the purchaser notice if you receive another offer for them to either confirm their purchase or let the deal go.

Sometimes your prospective buyer just may not have the money for a decent deposit, so you have to ask: What *other* security can you give me? What guarantees? Can you stagger the deposit i.e. pay it progressively until settlement?

What you're aiming to do (if you're selling in a hard market) is to find any way you can to improve the chances of this deal being completed, or getting something of value if it isn't.

Avoid the optimist's pattern of spending the proceeds of a sale before you get them

The risk you take when spending — or committing — the money before the deal settles is that you can find yourself in back-to-back settlements where a delay (or your buyer's failure to settle on your property) can put you under significant unnecessary pressure. When market prices go backwards it is *not* a time to be pushing the envelope or going hard out. A slower market is the time to build in more safety buffers on your deals — allow safety margins *especially* in your timeframes.

Remember that *pause* I referred to between the expansion and contraction parts of the cycle? Engineer some pauses, some space. Don't make things so tight and your steps so reliant on one another that a dispute or default by someone else immediately puts you under pressure in another corner, possibly even forcing you to sell into a down market rather than riding it out.

Late settlement — twelve working day period at the end of a contract

In a standard Sale & Purchase contract, if the buyer does not settle on time they have another twelve working days to do so. (How it works is that if the buyer doesn't meet settlement day, the vendor, usually through their solicitor, can serve a notice which gives the buyer a further twelve working days to settle.)

When the market gets difficult there will be more and more buyers using these twelve days. So, if as a seller you are banking on a deal settling on a certain date, remember these twelve days at the end of a contract give the buyer wriggle room* — unless you put in a clause in the contract that states that 'time is of the essence' which usually means that the twelve working days does not apply.

Even then, that clause can be challenged by a desperate buyer.*

When you're concerned that your purchaser might be a flight risk, or you have other concerns about them, be sure to put the 'time is of the essence' clause in the agreement and also increase the deposit as much as possible. Note the due performance dates of the contract in your diary and act immediately on any breach — if they do not pay the deposit (or an instalment of it) on time, serve a notice straight away. For non payment of the deposit you can usually serve a three working day notice on the buyer and if they do not pay you can cancel the contract.

This is the hard edge of the game; ride the conditions tightly. If they fail to perform on a timing issue, that's an indication that you may have to be careful. Act very fast on any early breach at the deposit stage, so that they are clear you won't tolerate any breaches of the agreement on settlement.

Being tight with them doesn't mean that you have to cancel their contract or be unreasonable but it keeps your options open and gives you choices to deal with difficult situations.

*Remember, if *you're* the desperate buyer you can use this wriggle room as well!

People get desperate, take short-cuts, and act out of integrity

Look below the surface. When buying property or doing business at this part of the cycle, things may not be as they seem.

As people get more desperate there are sometimes side agreements or deals that are hidden from public view. Some of these may be dubious, others downright illegal. Examine all paperwork carefully and do a thorough due diligence investigation on all parties to a lease, looking for real commercial relationships. Recently there's been publicity about fraudsters who provided lenders with altered valuation reports to support extra borrowing — more than the original valuation report recommended. The Institute of Valuers is advising funders to make sure they receive *original* valuation reports. The same applies for lease documents — ensure you have originals. (Sadly, this disreputable behaviour will only become more frequent as the pressure increases.)

A lease to a relative or associated company of the landlord is a red flag. Also, dig into the background of lease guarantors.

Most importantly, check that all rents are at market rents and certainly not more. It is common for some dubious vendors to increase rents to inflate the value. Look at market rents for what is (genuinely) being leased. How does that market rent compare to the passing rent? See Olly Newland's *The Rascal's Guide to Real Estate* for examples of dummy leases, tenants and buildings. Your best defence is *knowing* market rents.

Watch emotion and sentiment

As the market slides, the prevailing emotion moves from greed to fear. Under pressure, people become risk-averse, scared to move or take a risk. Some will sell at bargain prices just to relieve the pressure of the situation they're in — and that may be absolutely the right decision for them because the stress and emotional cost of staying in that situation is too high.

Get it in writing

A tight market can bring out the worst in people. In desperate circumstances, people's previous commitments mean less, or nothing at all. Others see an opportunity to exploit the pressure you're experiencing.

In real estate, as in any other business, you can often have a 'gentleman's agreement' in place. Based on past dealings with another party, you might have an understanding and expectation that certain things will eventuate. However, when the pressure comes on one party, suddenly they may no longer be a gentleman! Suddenly the ground has shifted and their perception and memory and interpretation of the situation has changed (usually in their favour). In order to defend yourself and your interests, ensure that you formalise any verbal agreements or understandings in writing. Get everything tied down. It will matter.

Parties look for ways out of deals and contracts by examining the fine print closely

Often there are ways out of even quite tightly written deals or contracts. Under pressure, some parties to an agreement will start looking for ways to escape from it. They have committed to a deal they can no longer honour.

Stressed buyers (and you might find yourself in this situation too) often look closely at the fine print of the contract (or get their lawyers to) seeking a way to renege on their commitment. They may try to find, for example, some condition the other party has not met, enabling them to say that the other party has not met their obligations, thus voiding the agreement. It may just be that they look for a way to put pressure on you to make a concession.

Of course, the same strategies are available to you if you are under pressure — examine the fine print of your agreement too. Be clear about what you and the other party have signed and see if there is any room for re-negotiation.

In every case, be very careful what you are signing before you sign it. Carefully check the fine print and have your advisors check it.

Poor credit behaviour — juggling creditors

As mentioned earlier, a common source of credit when people are under pressure is simply not to pay creditors on time. As property developments don't go well and people are squeezed, financial pressure will come to bear on a number of contractors and they won't be paid on time. When developers are struggling it is common for trades people and subcontractors not to be paid, or to be paid only a proportion of what they're due. Under pressure, any business will look at their bills, look at their available funds, and if their funds fall short, they'll work out who they *must* pay, who they can pay a little to, and who they can stall. In a pressure situation, people will juggle their financial commitments in this way.

How can this affect you? You might be paying your contractors on time, but their *other clients* might not be — which puts them under pressure to get money from *you* faster than they otherwise would. You pay your bills as normal, but you could get a call from your contractor saying that they have other people who are delaying their payments and as a result they're short of cash flow — 'Can you pay your bill early?' they ask. Otherwise they can't complete your work.

Be very careful in this situation because any such payment makes you, in effect, an unsecured creditor. If your contractor's business fails and you have paid them in advance it is highly unlikely you will see that money, or the promised goods or services, again.

If you choose not to (or cannot) pay your creditors on time you will have to deal with your creditors. It can be awful ringing creditors to tell them you can't pay them on time, or that you can only pay them a certain amount. As anxious as I was when I was in this position, I found that it worked much better to communicate openly with them so that they knew I was in a difficult situation. I found it far better to be honest, rather than stringing my creditors along and breaking a series of agreements.

I have had people in hard situations repeatedly breaking promises to me and it simply destroyed my trust in them — so that eventually I refused to work with them. Often, if you admit the situation, tell your creditors you can't pay on time but explain what you're working on, they will continue to support you to climb out of the hole. It is not a nice situation to be in — it's much better to avoid it — but if you find yourself in this situation, focus on dealing with it with integrity. Advise parties of broken agreements or the need to renegotiate as early as possible — then put in place agreements *you can keep* rather than making unrealistic promises just because you think that's what they want to hear.

10

Property development

Mike McCombie

I have done a great deal of property developing — sometimes successfully, but often not. Looking back, it almost seems as if I was acting to reinforce some past belief that 'life is a struggle'. Perhaps it's not *quite* that bad, but the down market presents a number of specific challenges, especially for developers.

Timing

Developing as the market drops, or trying to sell into a falling market, is not a great formula for making money. In fact, it's the opposite. At any given time, there are many developers in the market — and some have more experience than others.

In terms of the property cycle, the best time to develop is during the recovery phase, as the market starts to rise from the bottom of the slump. Doing it this way, you:

1) Acquire land for your project at the bottom of the cycle (when it is cheapest).

2) Carry out your development project when construction prices and margins are their slimmest, and then

3) Sell into a rising market, with increasing sale prices. This is the ideal.

However, many developers often enter the market at the bottom, successfully complete a small deal or a couple of small deals, then imagine they are experts, or bulletproof. In some cases they then carry on developing through to the top of the cycle, and beyond — but now with bigger deals (because now they see themselves as 'successful developers'). At or near the top of the cycle building costs always increase significantly. With lots of work available in the building industry, both labour and material costs rise, as do contractors' margins and professional fees. All of this combines to make property developments less economic and more marginal.

Sometimes these new developers' timing leads them to take on their biggest deal yet, since they want to play a bigger game, but sadly:

1) They often pay top price for the land.

2) Construction costs have boomed.

3) Things take longer than they forecast.

4) By the time they're selling, they're doing it into a market where the prices and demand are dropping and costs of funds are higher — all making it much harder to achieve sales and to get their prices.

Also, the risk of some of their pre-sales failing to settle is greater. A pre-sale is a Sale & Purchase agreement, often sold at a discount on full value, put in place prior to construction to get sufficient sales in place to meet the funders' repayment requirements. In harder times lenders get nervous and they look much more closely at those pre-sales, sometimes demanding full details of every buyer because the lenders have been burned by cowboys and fraudsters in the guise of developers. Overall, it becomes a *much* more difficult game.

Many developers also get an unpleasant introduction to 'the developer's squeeze'. Construction prices escalate, delays and interest bills balloon and construction costs blowout—then the units don't sell for the expected prices. The profit margin becomes narrower and is sometimes extinguished completely.

Once the market starts turning, many developers find that not only will they not *make* any money from their projects, worse, they'll lose money. In some cases deals aren't completed and there are forced sales at bargain prices.

This can be a worthwhile investment opportunity if you are cashed up. However, a word of caution is necessary as there can be (and usually are) significant underlying issues to be resolved in failed developments which you might inherit with the project. Picking the bones of a partially-completed development is not an undertaking for inexperienced investors.

Exposure to other businesses' failure

When developing, your head contractor can go under part-way through your contract. This can have a severe impact on your project timing and completion (not to mention debt-funding). Particularly at a down time in the market, be sure you don't overpay your contractors or pay them in advance. If you have paid them too much and they go under, as I mentioned earlier, you will never see that money again.

Also, make sure your head contractor has paid the sub-contractors before you pay them any more money for the next stage. Funders who follow sound lending practice often require proof of this (or they should) before they authorise the next draw-down. In one of our developments the head contractor was paid but didn't pay the subcontractors. Once the head contractor's business dissolved, the subcontractors came back to us, the developer, with highly-inflated quotes to complete the project (knowing we were under intense pressure). They got away with this blackmail because we had no other real option. The potential negative effect on building warranties if the subcontractors were changed part-way through the project was a significant motivating factor in our decision to accept the subcontractors' offer. (This was another case of a pressure situation bringing out the worst in people.)

Minimise your risks

Manage your development projects tightly and monitor all costs closely. It is critical that you have tight management systems in place when undertaking any development project. I always use a project manager whose role it is to certify and sign off on payments. I only pay those certified payments and make sure retentions are held back. I am diligent in constantly updating the records of costs to complete the project; this ensures that I have the funds to complete the project.

It is incredibly detailed work and not my area of expertise which is why I use someone who is appropriately qualified and aware of the pitfalls.

Overall, be very wary of developing on the down cycle. It's much better to start near the bottom or just on the upside.

Beware the cowboys

People who take short-cuts (the cowboys) are badly exposed when the market turns. That's the season for collapsing development and construction companies, subcontractors, finance companies, and second-tier lenders. The trouble starts with the cowboys but unfortunately spreads to affect even sound operators.

Last time there was a significant downturn in the economy, in 1987, there were a number of second-tier funders who had been lending large sums of money to developers at terrific interest rates; however, in a number of cases they had been taking short-cuts. In essence, these lenders were not doing what they were meant to in terms of obtaining security for their investors, nor were they carrying out proper due diligence on the projects they were funding. Sometimes they were lending to associated parties on favourable terms.

When things tighten up and confidence drops, these finance companies' bonds (repayable to their investors) come due, but of course there isn't the inflow of new funds that they'd been relying on. Next, one or two developers go under and default on their loans — and soon that lender is in trouble. Watch out for frantic advertising and increasingly attractive yields offered by these finance houses who are trying to shore up the outflow with fresh money. It is important to realise that it's getting riskier and riskier to put your money anywhere near them, as the Reserve Bank has warned.

As I write, there have been a number of finance company collapses with more rumoured to be on the way — and increasing TV advertisements for finance companies seeking funds.

People and businesses who have been taking short-cuts are exposed and cleaned out. Remember, as unpleasant as it is, this is one of the functions of the down part of the cycle — to eliminate waste.

Some property syndicates and companies will collapse

When the pressure increases there will be some property-related company collapses — often affecting those who do not understand the market or have been hiding things.

It's terrible if you're caught by one of these collapses, but this situation can offer great opportunities for others.

If you are invested in a property company or a syndicate, make sure your money is protected. Watch the debt levels and look for a spread of cash flow — not just one major investment that could go awry. If you are not comfortable with your investment for any reason, *get out* immediately or as early as you can arrange it.

It is especially important to manage the re-tenanting of syndicated property when leases are coming to an end. As with any commercial property, and as I have detailed above, selling a vacant property under pressure at the bottom of the cycle is a great way to lose equity, and money, fast.

11

Actions you can take to protect yourself

Mike McCombie

What actions should you take to protect yourself before prices start really falling and the market corrects? Here are a few suggestions based on my experience and knowledge.

Examine your vulnerable points and sensitivities

Ask yourself where could the pressure come from? How might it look? How intense could it be? And, most importantly, what can I do to protect myself from it? *Now.*

Is it going to be a recession? Or worse, will it be a depression? If so, what do I need to do, firstly, to survive, and secondly to prosper? Think about these things. Make plans.

The key here is to act early, and ideally to set yourself up when the market is strong, because the further into a slump you leave it the harder things will be to turn around.

Before prices start going backwards, when you get that intuitive feeling that the market is going to correct, examine your financial situation and identify where you are vulnerable. Where are your pressure points? What are your sensitivities?

Many investors are vulnerable due to poor cash flow combined with too much debt. A strategy for these circumstances is to sell property, especially your lower quality or vacant buildings and land, sooner rather than later, to reduce your debt and strengthen your cash flow.

Before one slump I remember being a bit tight on cash flow but not wanting to sell a building because I might have to pay tax on some of the proceeds. I read Prechter's *Conquer the Crash* (a great book for reviewing the prospect of a global depression and what to do) and was cured of my reservations by one of his statements. He counsels not to let concerns about paying tax influence your decisions about whether to sell property. If it will protect your position, then it may be the right time to sell. He points out that if you are later forced to sell into a depressed market at prices say 20% to 30% lower than the peak then all of your tax problems will be over because you won't have any profits to pay tax on anyway!

Needless to say, I sold.

Stay aware

Look at trends, read the news, digest market information (interest rates, vacancy rates, bank attitudes, demand for different types of property) and listen to what people are saying. Filter information to become aware of what things could mean for your own financial situation. Ask yourself: What could this mean for the economy? What will the affect be on my tenants? And how will my investments be affected?

You will hear lots of noise — often conflicting. For example, a bank might report record year-end profits but at the *same time* forecast a slump in projected profits. What's relevant?

Ask yourself 'What if?' questions. 'What if this did (or didn't) happen?', 'Am I safe?', 'How likely is it?' and

'Do I need to do anything about this now to protect myself or set myself up to take advantage of it?'

Read and educate yourself on this subject *before* it happens. As mentioned, *Conquer The Crash* by Robert Prechter is worth reading, as is *The Day the Bubble Bursts* by Olly Newland (see recommended reading).

Clean up all your messes

During 1987 I had lots of unresolved issues that I failed to address. This neglect of my investments ultimately caused even greater problems. As a result, I have learnt to clean up any issues in the present time i.e. debts paid on time, renovations fully completed, documentation completed. I aim to keep things in order as best I can.

I remember being surprised one day when my bank manager at Westpac said to me, "Developers have tails."

He meant that developers have outstanding issues to resolve and complete at the end of each deal. I was surprised, I thought this was a secret closely held by developers, but now I was hearing that my bank manager knew! In my experience it is very true. These details are the tails that can often get pulled, stood on, even jammed in the door, when the market turns.

If you have some messes, clean them up before a downturn. It is easier to do then, rather than waiting until the property cycle turns. If possible, repay any non-serviced debt, and non-productive debt like personal, credit card, and consumer debt.

Liquidate your lower quality stock

Sell up fringe property, property that is harder to let, or vacant buildings and bare land, as these are the worst affected in a slump, they can be a liability since usually they don't earn income. Different sorts of property are affected differently as the market turns. Remember at the top of the market there is often minimal (if any) discount for risk and secondary properties sell at top prices still, due to demand. There's much more of a discount on these once the market has turned. As the market slides, it becomes harder to get tenants for fringe property so the premises sit vacant for longer. Vacant property is a liability, hence the risk premium increases. When cash flow is tight and the slump places pressure on the market's players, you can buy land very cheaply. (Prior to the slump, there are optimists who will pay incredibly high prices for land.) Use the proceeds of the sale to retire debt, strengthen your cash flow, improve your financial position, and lower your debt-to-equity ratio. The ultimate aim should be to have your debt-to-equity ratio between 50% and 60% or lower if you are concerned about a major correction. If at all possible, create a buffer on cash flow to support vacancies and increased holding costs. By doing this you make yourself more attractive to lenders.

Upgrade your portfolio with better properties that will weather the storm more comfortably (e.g. better locations, better tenants, longer leases). Ridding yourself of marginal quality property and holding on to better options makes it more likely you'll be untouched (or survive) when the economy tests your investments.

Essentially, *strengthen your portfolio.*

Be careful of provincial properties

Often provincial properties feel the benefits of the boom *last*, but the impact of the downturn *first*. These markets can also sometimes go down faster and recover much more slowly. The market is a lot thinner in small towns and rural areas, so if your tenant leaves, it can be hard to replace them.

Olly Newland tells the story of a friend of his who was badly burnt when he bought the only factory in a rural town, thinking the firm that was his tenant had been there for generations and had no plans to move. They shut it down shortly after the deal went through — what did the vendor know that he hadn't shared? — and the new owner wasn't able to find a replacement tenant for the factory, ever.

Do the paperwork

Get all lease documentation completed and formalised (i.e. leases, lease renewals, assignments of lease, rent reviews, etc.) Take defensive action *early* and complete and formalise documentation to reduce 'misunderstandings' that may occur when difficult times arise.

Tie down tenants and make your relationship with them stronger so they are more likely to stay with you. Find out what they need to make them more satisfied with your premises and, if reasonable, find a way to do it for them. Drop rental rates if absolutely necessary so you have income coming in, though beware the subsequent drop in your building's value. It's preferable to find other ways to keep your tenants rather than offering them straight rent reduction.

If you have to drop the rent, find some other way to package it. (Use a rent holiday, fitout assistance or some other arrangement which leaves the actual passing annual rent figure intact for valuation purposes.) However, at the end of the day it may still be worth sacrificing some rental income if this will secure your tenant longer term through a hard time.

Crucially, concentrate on servicing your existing tenants well. Keep the lines of communication open. As mentioned earlier, other landlords with vacant buildings will want your tenants, so keep your tenants happy and look for ways to lock them in for longer.

More important paperwork

Get your legal and ownership structures (family trusts or trading trusts, LAQCs etc) set up and working properly — or reviewed — so that your various assets are separated and ring-fenced. Protect your core assets. Do what needs to be done to avoid a house-of-cards-type collapse. Separate mortgages from different lenders enable you to keep problems with one property (you may have lost a tenant, for example) from affecting others. Note that there are time limits within which asset disposals can be clawed back after they have been sold or transferred to trusts — so do the restructuring sooner rather than later to get this timeframe out of the way as early as possible.

Laws and case law relating to legal structures, related parties etc are constantly changing. The government, the IRD, and sometimes creditors can challenge these trusts and structures by seeking to go behind them. Also, be aware that your arrangement of structures may date and need revising. It may no longer provide the protection it once did. Stay up-to-date. Have a good accountant and good lawyer *with relevant property experience* advise you. If there are pressure points that need protecting, pay the money and take the action.

If you have a number of properties financed with one lender, refinance them with *different* lenders — and, as already mentioned, avoid cross-collateralised loans. Like you, lenders will be trying to improve their position as the market turns, to improve their security. Be sure to only give them what you must. Try to maintain some unencumbered property or property with decent equity for future borrowing.

Set some funds aside

Set yourself up so that you have spare cash (ideally) or at least good accessible equity (a property with very low borrowings and with strong cash flow so that when (inevitable) opportunities arise in a down market you can move quickly. A very successful investor we know in Brisbane always keeps one unencumbered income-producing asset in his portfolio so that when opportunities arise he can move quickly.

Do some self-improvement

Improve your knowledge and skills — both the analytical (number-crunching and knowledge-based) and the so-called 'soft skills' such as negotiating, communication, listening, etc.

Develop, tighten and fine-tune your policies, your investing rules, your criteria for handling a deal, your procedures and systems. Read widely, studying the market here and overseas. Get ready to lift your game. Take a look at your team and be prepared to upgrade it if necessary. If you have done all this and the market still hasn't turned and it is too difficult to find deals, then go fishing and wait.

12

Strategies for investing in a low market

Mike McCombie

Consciously create your future and your vision

Before and during the correction, develop and hold your *own* vision of how the market will treat you rather than adopting the generally prevailing view, which will be negative. (Robert Kiyosaki once said, "We are always either selling our vision of reality or buying someone else's.")

At the bust or bottom of the slump the overwhelming sentiment is negative. Some unfortunate people will have lost large amounts of money, the media will be negative, headlines will convey doom and gloom, catastrophe. Far from its boom-time status of 'flavour of the month, there'll be a 'crisis warning' attitude toward property — with 'don't go there' or 'my brother-in-law lost a fortune in property' stories in abundance.

Create a positive statement for yourself, something like: 'There are great bargains to be had and I am in a position to take advantage of them.' Reinforce this for yourself.

My own vision is that we will not only survive but do phenomenally well in the next correction. There will be incredibly good deals and we will buy good-quality property genuinely undervalued.

Develop your 'practice'

So you have a positive and empowering vision of your financial world to see you through the slump. Is this enough?

No.

It is true that vision precedes all action — but it is no *substitute* for action. It's not just enough to have a vision, as you need to take action, consistently, over time, to develop an investment 'practice'. I'm using the word practice slightly differently, so let me explain what I mean using yoga as an example.

My wife and I practice yoga and have done for over ten years. I learned early on that I can read books on yoga, I can think about it, dream about it, and talk to my friends about it — *but* if I am not getting on my mat *physically* doing my yoga practice most days, then none of that other stuff counts. I won't get anywhere. That *practice* is what I need to do daily. (And incidentally, yoga serves me very well as a counter-balance to my property investing, helping me deal with stress and bringing a whole lot of other benefits. Try it.)

The practice is what I do day by day, week by week, year by year — taking me towards my goal, in this case financial freedom. It's the stuff that takes me towards my vision.

I hear from lots of people about them wanting to be wealthy property investors but they do not have a financial practice — and that's how one achieves the results. Others I see start a practice then stop.

So examine the state of your financial practice. What are you doing? Where are you focused? How do you spend your time? The answers to these questions will show you how much you value the goal.

Keeping going after a mistake

When a property investor makes a mistake, it usually comes out of the back pocket. Money, real money, is lost! You literally 'pay' for your mistakes.

I see many people who, when they make a mistake, stop practising. They give up.

Others stop when the practice gets hard, or they reach a plateau. Any worthwhile pursuit will have challenges, any journey has plateaus, and it is important to *keep going* because if you do, you will move through the plateau over time to the next level, in this case, a new level of more wealth.

The challenge when you make a mistake or when it gets hard is to *keep the practice going*.

When the market gets hard, when you're not getting the results you want, go back and focus on your vision — and *keep your practice going*. When things start going bad, many investors start focusing on what I call 'pathology' (what's dead and dying e.g. the lost money or the failed deals). Unfortunately, this habit has a tendency to attract more of the same into their lives.

Learn from your mistakes. Ask: 'What have I learned from what just happened?' And *keep going with your practice*.

Return to your vision of how it's going to be for you ('there are great bargains to be had and I am in a position to take advantage of them'). Hold on to it. *Keep practising*.

This is not new age mumbo-jumbo, it's some of the most valuable advice I can give you.

Understand the game

Remember how I mentioned that I went bust because of greed and ignorance? I was ignorant because I did not fundamentally understand the game and how it would change as the cycle and the market moved.

I am amazed at the number of people who want to play the game of commercial property investing (especially in boom times) who fundamentally do not understand how it works.

The more you understand the game of investing and in particular commercial property investing, with its various machinations, in both boom and slump times, the better prepared you will be to take advantage of any correction.

Put the effort into educating yourself. (See recommended reading and visit www.EmpowerEducation.com)

Be cashed up and ready to buy — cash is king

A common question is: should we cash up and just sit idle during a good market? Or should we still be investing and growing while the market goes backwards?

Increasingly *cash will be king*. Make sure you have cash. As asset prices slide back, the buying power of cash effectively increases, and you will find it becomes essential to have some.

Even though you are not doing anything with that cash, as a slump begins the value of your cash increases. So it may be that the best investment you can make is to hold onto your cash and get a return from wherever you have it (securely) placed, because its buying power is growing.

This should be balanced by your continued practice of looking for deals — if you find a really good deal, act on it. (For example, if you can buy a mortgagee sale property for say, two-thirds of valuation, that probably gives you enough of a safety buffer to be a good deal.) Keep an eye on the market for those really good deals and do them.

Target distressed or 'high need' vendors or those who just want to get out for some reason:

- Banks or mortgagees trying to get rid of 'under-performing' loans.

- Deceased estates — where sometimes the beneficiaries are more interested in a hasty, easy sale than getting the last dollar of value.

- Marriage splits — where an agenda other than maximising the price received from the sale can be driving the deal.

- Poorly-managed properties.

At or near the bottom of the cycle property, companies that were over-geared (such as mutual funds, trusts and corporates) quite often sell a property because it's not performing. Sometimes it's worse — they are collapsing. Or they could just be trying to raise cash.

In a strong market, many of the properties for sale are very well presented — vendors have lots of money and values are up. But at the bottom of the cycle properties are often very poorly presented. Dispirited or desperate vendors sometimes self-sabotage, seeming to have no energy or money to renovate or even tidy up their buildings and they put them on the market in shocking condition. (Don't do this yourself if you're ever selling under pressure!) Likewise, commercial landlords having trouble with their tenants can lose interest or even give up, and their lease documentation can be years out of date. This is a great opportunity to buy and add value.

In a slump there will be lots of opportunities to pick up badly presented properties which are usually (but not always) indicative of a high-need vendor. Look around for that sort of property (and vendor) and be patient.

Do not put yourself under pressure — don't be a latecomer to the party. Don't be so impressed by stories of other people's success that you stupidly join in as the party is ending. Robert Kiyosaki's wisdom is useful here: "We have all missed booms. A wise investor knows to wait for the next boom, rather than jump in if they've missed the current one." Be patient, yet stay ready to move quickly. Don't rush in, wait until things are at, or near, or *past* the bottom.

Buy long as a strategy

In a low market, buy long — be prepared to buy and hold until the market changes for the better. Aim to ride the market or cycle up. Get the double-whammy of increased rentals and lowering yields (increased values) working for you. Review the example earlier of the potential drop in value through the cycle but imagine it going the other way. You can make phenomenal gains doing this.

Beware of vacant properties, allow much more time to find tenants and allow more contingency for holding costs. If you have a vacant property or are looking to buy one, they can be really cheap to acquire (somebody is selling you their problem) but allow lots of time and ensure you have made it a really good deal as it may well still be hard for you to find tenants when the economic cycle is at a low. Often it's a good strategy to find a tenant first, then a building that suits them. The value is in the tenant.

Buy well

Focus on undervalued or add-value opportunities. Remember, you make your money when you buy, even if you don't 'realise' it until you sell. If you buy well everything gets easier from there. If you pay too much settling the deal things can get harder.

If you are in a strong position and the opportunity comes up to acquire a long term strategic hold — one of those really well-located prime properties — do it. They are cheaper in the slump.

Look for property that has been on the market for a long time e.g. a building with a faded old real estate sign or an old sign with a new one beside it. Look to see if the real estate agency has changed. Vendors can often take some time to be conditioned by the market, and in a hard market owners *hate* to give up and sell their properties at a loss. People do not like realizing their losses. They resist it. Give them time to get used to the idea. It can take six months for the vendor's mindset and attitude to be altered from the optimism of their initial listing. When they first put the property on the market they would never have entertained your offer — after a while with it sitting unsold, they may be much more realistic and flexible.

Look at what has been sitting on the market for a while and revisit it. You can often pick up great bargains or deals this way. Also the conditions you can negotiate at that stage can be fantastic compared to the high of a seller's market.

In a low market, you can often get the non-price negotiating items: delayed settlement, access to renovate, vendor finance — these things can literally make the deal possible. Work on vendor conditions that are more favourable to you, as there will be fewer interested buyers. The whole power equation has changed: you, as the buyer, have the power. There is much more flexibility around the non-price negotiating toward the bottom end of the market.

When considering a prospective purchase, look at the quality of the tenant, and the industry they are in. How are they likely to be affected by a downturn? e.g. Do they sell luxury items or staples? Or are they in a more transient, less stable business? As with any commercial purchase, look at the existing lease terms carefully. (As we advise in *Commercial Real Estate Investor's Guide*, read the lease terms line-by-line.)

Get in the deal stream again and play

In the slump, it's important to get in the deal stream again. There will be a constant flow of deals. What can be difficult is that the pervading sentiment will be negative. As Olly Newland says, "it's *hard* to buy when everyone else is heading for the exits."

Start.

Jump back in and look for deals at the bottom end of the market when the negativity is still there. Play with a few deals. See if you can find an irresistible one. Don't be afraid to kick a few tyres. It's just a numbers game and the more deals you look at, the more likely it will be that sooner or later one will pop up that is a really good buy — but not if you don't look.

Keep the big picture in mind

Look at how any particular deal you're considering would affect your overall position. Ask: will this strengthen my position? Or will it put me under too much pressure?

Look at the individual deal and see whether (1) it's a good deal on its own — but (more?) importantly (2) also look at what impact owning that property will have on your whole financial position. If a deal puts your overall financial position at risk, let it go — even if it appears to be a good deal on its own. Pass it on to someone else (for a fee if possible). Keep your big picture in mind.

Do your numbers thoroughly. A tight market is no time to find you have miscalculated and your position isn't as good as you thought it was. Run the calculations *carefully* and have someone else check them if you're not sure. Be very thorough in your paperwork and allow for contingencies.

Look out for the non-financial parts of your life

First things first: look after yourself and your loved ones.

Examine the non-financial parts of your life and honestly assess these. Look after your primary relationship, your family, and your health. Try to be in the strongest position possible when the pressure comes on at the bottom of the cycle.

Some people (it could be you!) will be working long hours to try to retrieve their financial position. They drop into 'survival mode'. In some cases their health, family or marriage falls apart.

Keep an eye on your health and if you have one, your primary relationship. Keep time aside for your family and your partner. This is crucial. You do not want a marriage break-up, or emotional or health issues to affect you, particularly when you're under financial pressure at the low end of the cycle. Being forced to sell assets at that time will seriously reduce their sale value — adding to your woes.

Let's face it, in boom times there can be a real shortage of good deals — and far too many people willing to pay too much for them. So why not use this part of the cycle and the first part of the slump to work and play with other things? Go for balance!

During the last upwards correction I heard a bank manager giving advice on the radio that buoyant times were a great time to be working on your intimate relationship. He pointed out: you really don't want to be going through a marriage split (with a subsequent forced sale of assets) when values are falling — or worse at the bottom of the cycle. This is sage advice.

The same goes for your health, your family, your spirituality (things which feed your spirit) and the whole of your life. As far as possible, get things into a calm and stable position in your life so that if there is a financial correction or collapse coming, you are as well-prepared as possible and can meet it with equanimity.

Emotional stress

Under pressure some people panic, some become overwhelmed or freeze into inaction and paralysis. If you have made mistakes or been caught out it's no good being stuck in denial, blame, or justification — start by taking responsibility for what has happened and proactively look for the best course of action from where you are now. Being stuck on how it 'used to look' will get you nowhere. Ask: what do I need to do to go forward from where I am now?

Forewarned is forearmed

I haven't covered this to depress you, but to warn you. A slump in the market is not all bleak, nor is it all death and destruction. But it's important to be conscious about what *can* go wrong. There is much more chance of things going wrong when the market falls back, because that's when the pressure increases. Our goal for the information presented in these pages is to help you make sure it doesn't go wrong for you. If you truly want to survive and prosper then pay attention to the advice and tips in this book. If it is a minor correction then you will sail through. If it is a major one, you will weather the storm and be in a position to buy great deals along the way.

Last words — tithe and contribute

Get in the habit of tithing money and time. Also look at how you can contribute something of the skills and abundance you have.

I remember when I had nothing and was starting to rebuild, every time I gave either time or money to a worthwhile cause, things went more smoothly for me in my business dealings. I was amazed. Tenants appeared, great deals came along and were accepted, funding fell into place. All manner of support came back to me. This is still my experience today.

Most people have to continually work to handle their financial survival. If you become a successful property investor then you will have wealth handled. I encourage you to set yourself up financially and look at how you can create healthy, beautiful visions for yourself, your loved ones and your community — and put your energy towards creating those.

Mike McCombie's DVD set *Proven Formulas for Investing in Commercial Real Estate* is available from www.EmpowerEducation.com

13

Survive and prosper in times of financial adversity

Mark Withers

Financial adversity can be broadly split into two categories: the macro environment — the 'big picture' economic situation — and the micro environment, where the challenges are specific to you as an individual, family, or business. Times of adversity in a macro sense are often aligned with economic factors. The property cycle is essentially an economic phenomenon that recognises the cyclical pattern of good times following bad.

For you to prosper from this cycle as an investor or homeowner, it's useful to recognise its stages and make sure you're in a position to operate 'counter-cyclically' (against the trend) e.g. by acquiring assets when the cycle is in a downward pattern — and conversely, being able to afford to hold assets when cycles (values and costs) are trending up. These are two fairly well understood strategies associated with prospering from whatever the current macro-economic climate might be.

The real skill comes in (1) setting oneself up to take advantage of these macro opportunities as they emerge and (2) having the courage to act.

Micro adversity on the other hand, can be to some extent self-inflicted — e.g. poor decision making and bad planning — but external influences can bring times of adversity that have a significant effect on one's investing success and wealth creation plan.

Let's examine some of these micro situations and see what strategies and lessons we can take from them.

Financial

The cardinal sin of the property investor is to become over-committed. Over-commitment generally takes the form of borrowing too much money — borrowing to a point where your income isn't able to sustain servicing of the debt. Property investors should recognise that the ability to retain their assets has got very little to do with the overall value of them, or even their equity in them, but much more to do with their ability to sustain cash flow in times of adversity.

When interest rates rise significantly (which is part of the economic cycle), many property investors make the assumption that they'll be able to increase rents to keep pace with this. Nothing could be further from the truth! We should *all* remember that our tenants also carry debt. Their debt is often the most expensive type — e.g. hire purchase and finance company-type debts which are extremely burdensome. In times of adversity, tenants can often afford *less* for rent, rather than more. As a landlord you will often see tenants looking for cheaper accommodation in tough times. So it's a mistake for an investor to assume their increased interest costs can be passed directly on to the tenant.

Let's be honest. If you do find yourself in an over-committed situation, and efforts to increase income have failed, there is only one strategy to get out from under and that is to sell assets. Every time an asset is sold an investor's loan-to-value ratio will improve, assuming all of the funds from the disposal are applied to the reduction of the debt. (This will generally be what must happen by virtue of bank lending criteria.) If any of your assets are cross-collateralised, you should not assume that cash from the sale of them will become available. If your lender is in a position to further reduce their debt and can do so because some of your debts are cross-collateralised against other assets you can be fairly sure they'll grab the bag — especially if they feel you're not in a strong position.

A good piece of advice: if you are in a situation of having to sell, recognise that the inevitable is approaching and act *well before* your hand is forced by the bank. In almost every situation, the outcome is likely to be far better if you can deal with the sale of the property yourself, rather than waiting for the bank to foreclose on it. You may even enhance your reputation with your lender if you're seen to have been able to take action and manage the situation yourself rather than simply implode into an ugly mortgagee sale situation.

Divorce or other matrimonial split

Divorce is another micro adversity factor that can have a massive impact on one's wealth and investing potential. Divorce now extends not only to married people but, through legislation, also to de facto and civil union couples.

Essentially, the law says that once a relationship has become akin to marriage (after three years), assets must be divided 50/50 in the event of separation. This means that people can unexpectedly find themselves being legislatively directed *as if they are married* when they may have had no intention of mingling their affairs to that extent.

There are some strategies associated with managing the risks of a relationship split.

Clearly, this book is not designed to give marital advice but it is fair to say that a broken marriage is one of the most devastating things that can occur, affecting your wealth building and asset retention. It strikes me as a great shame that so many people are so willing to invest time and money in learning strategies to build wealth, but seem unwilling to spend anywhere near the same time or money investing in their own relationships.

I believe that a successful person will have a strategy to build and enhance their marriage or relationship to give themselves the best possible chance of achieving not only personal happiness but also long-term wealth. In many ways, a perfect marriage or perfect relationship is also the perfect platform for wealth creation. The division of duties amongst the couple, whether income-producing or family management, often creates the time and resources required to build wealth. In my experience, the old saying of two being more powerful than one is very true — and a good relationship builds a platform that enables prosperity to blossom as the relationship strengthens.

It's inescapable that some relationships fail for whatever reason, and so it can be prudent to take steps to deal with that impact on one's investments and wealth.

Asset protection

Single people who have been able to create wealth (or who have perhaps inherited it) should look to take some steps towards protecting their assets prior to forming long-term relationships or entering marriages. Many people assume that all they are required to do is create a family trust to place assets in and this will in some way be a cure-all or silver bullet to protect their assets should their relationship fail. This is definitely *not* the case.

A *family trust* is a step in the right direction. Vesting property in the trust will effectively separate those assets from your personal name, but the ability to transfer assets into a trust is limited to $27,000 a year of gifting unless you're prepared to pay gift duty to the Inland Revenue Department (IRD). The thresholds for gifting have not been altered for decades and so now with the median house price over $400,000 the ability to move wealth quickly from your personal name into a trust simply does not exist.

Entering into a *relationship agreement* prior to the relationship becoming classed as a matrimonial one and the assets consequently becoming relationship property is another pivotal component to protecting your assets in case of a split. This agreement — which 'contracts out' of the Property (Relationships) Act — would normally follow a discussion with your partner about their willingness to enter into a relationship agreement. Raising this subject can be a social taboo — and I believe that's why many people don't do it. The parties to the relationship are simply too nervous about raising these issues. This attitude must change. There's too much at stake *not* to have this conversation.

For example, a female client for whom I am a trustee told me about a new relationship that she was enjoying. We discussed her assets and that the trust still owed her money and that this debt to her was a personal asset. I recommended that she should sit down that evening after dinner and have a discussion with her new boyfriend about his willingness to sign a relationship agreement that acknowledged that her property was separate property and would never be considered relationship property. She agreed to do that.

The following morning, I received an emotional phone call from my client saying her relationship had ended the previous evening! She told me this had happened because her partner had fundamentally objected to any suggestion that he should participate in a relationship agreement. She felt that she had no option but to end the relationship and was grief-stricken as a result. Sure, this was an extremely difficult situation to cope with personally, but she could see it was far better for her to have realised this before the relationship had lasted long enough for him to have laid a claim to 50% of her assets! She was grateful that I'd pushed her to have the discussion.

Child support

Another issue associated with a relationship split is the effects and consequences if there are dependent children. In this situation the partner who does not have custody of the children is expected to pay child support via the IRD — a 'liable parent contribution'. This contribution is a portion of income which is diverted to the partner with custody to ensure that there is a balance in the care and upbringing of the children.

The payment of child support is a significant burden on someone who is, generally speaking, trying to re-establish themself. In many cases, the requirement to divert what can be a significant portion of income into child support can spell the end to an investment strategy, if that strategy requires the maximisation of income. The amount of time and energy some people spend trying to *avoid their commitments* to child support is a disgrace — and frankly, a great shame when the same time and energy has not been spent maintaining and fostering a positive relationship that could have led to prosperity rather than adversity.

Personal health

Health problems also come into the category of micro adversity, threatening income. In New Zealand we all contribute to and enjoy the benefits of accident compensation. The accident compensation system is designed to ensure that those suffering injury are compensated by ACC for as long as it takes to re-enter the workforce and re-establish one's income. ACC payments are based on the incomes that are lost as a result of the accident, with contributions also based on the level of one's personal income.

While the ACC system does ensure that income levels are maintained through adversity caused by accident, ACC is not designed to cover illness. It surprises me that more people do not take steps to insure (a) their health and (b) their income. Falling ill and being unable to work is a hugely significant threat to maintaining and building one's personal wealth. Stop and contemplate for a moment how long it would be before you would run out of money — and be forced to default on a mortgage — if you got sick and were unable to work.

I recall a situation where an accountant colleague of mine was diagnosed with an eye problem that ultimately resulted in a cornea transplant. As his sight failed he was unable to work as an accountant and suffered significant adversity because he hadn't insured his income. In many cases, income protection policies are also tax deductible. (This is not always the case, particularly where policies are of an agreed value irrespective of actual declared income.) A specialist risk insurance broker will be able to advise on the best income protection policy for your needs. Don't ignore it.

Any discussion about health must also extend to life insurance. As you become wealthier it is fair to say that the need for life insurance can diminish. If, for instance, your net income from assets has reached the point where all your outgoings could be serviced and debts repaid even in the event of the death of your partner, you need less. In these circumstances your requirement to insure your life to a point where debts can be reduced or cleared may not be quite as important. But if you have a young family or the traditional arrangement of a working spouse with the other at home, it's probably very sensible to insure the life of both, but in particular the income earner, so that in the event of death, there are sufficient funds to clear debt to a level where remaining assets can be retained.

Having said this, I believe it is important not to over-insure. The costs of life insurance grow as we age and if there's no absolute need for this insurance (i.e. it's not a requirement of a mortgage) the income that is being diverted into it might be better directed into debt reduction or other investments. Find a way to strike a balance.

•••

Financial strategies to profit from adversity

We have a saying in the accounting world: 'You should never make a decision until you have got the facts, got the facts, and got the facts.' This maxim is based around good planning and good information gathering — so that good decisions can be made.

Property investment is generally a fairly safe activity, but there is a natural human tendency to move on to 'bigger and better' things. I like to use the analogy of the game of Snakes and Ladders.

If every time your assets grow in value, you leverage again to a point where your borrowing power is maximised (i.e. borrow as much as you can), you are taking on *more and more* risk with your investment. If one of those investments

---

is not properly planned or creates adversity, it is potentially possible to ride the 'snake' from your existing position all the way back to start again because of the effect of forced sales. Staying with a game analogy, the 'domino effect' can see you lose much more than you thought you had at risk — and much more quickly. I've seen it happen. The ride back up tends to be a series of small 'ladders'. One good investment will lead to another and another to another.

Stick to what you know

Experience suggests one of the most successful strategies for building and maintaining wealth is to stick to a theme. Stick to what you know. This is absolutely essential for those contemplating property development and property trading activities. The nature of the property trader and developer is that they love the thrill of the deal. In my observation, if the deals get bigger and bigger, it is only a matter of time before something goes wrong and they ride the snake back to the start again.

As a strategy for success, I suggest this: build your skill levels and try to do lots of deals of a similar nature until you have mastered these transactions, then move *gradually* into more complicated activities. Don't ever give in to the temptation to enter a deal where you don't really have the skills to succeed.

Do the sums

I've been shocked to witness many situations where property developers acquire properties without undertaking proper due diligence and really proving to themselves *financially* and *mathematically* that there is actually an upside to the deal. It is purely reckless to purchase properties when you are not certain of the overall financial outcomes — but people do it.

I am also surprised by people who invest time and money setting up financial structures to separate property investing from property trading activities but still end up chopping and changing after acquisition. Usually they say this is because they've decided that the 'trading' property would in fact be best kept as an investment property or vice versa. There's no excuse for this in my view. It's simply an indication of extremely poor planning and bad financial judgment. There will be consequences.

Avoid over-commitment

Another trap is the desire to pounce on what might appear to be a golden opportunity before you have completed an existing project which requires your attention. People who do this become over-extended before they've achieved the outcome enabling them to move forward in a less risky manner. Do *not* be tempted to take on more projects before you have attained the goal you expect from the project you are already working on.

As the saying goes: 'The deal of the century comes up once a week.' If you have to pass up a good deal to remain focused on the work that you already have in hand, this is a sign of good discipline. Console yourself with the thought that there will be plenty of opportunities out there to pursue once you have completed the work that you are doing.

Do not rush your acquisitions

Through my work as a chartered accountant, I've seen many people come into property investment with bundles of enthusiasm and passion. Sometimes they rush the process. They set themselves ambitious goals; for example, to buy one property a year for ten years, and think that this is in some way a small goal.

In my view, the acquisition of more than one good quality property per year as a long term property investor (unless you're *full-time* at it) is, in my view, an aggressive goal. For many part-time investors, it will be a significant challenge to achieve. Setting a goal like this can sometimes lead the investor to rush the acquisition process — especially if their personal income is restricted. There is a limit to how much money banks will lend. If you rush out and acquire properties too quickly and use up all your available borrowing power, the *really special* deals that don't come up every year may pass you by because you have filled your portfolio with mediocre or low income-producing property investments.

Set rules and criteria

Ideally, you want to retain your ability to buy another property but at the same time set some financial criteria which enable you to determine exactly what constitutes a suitable acquisition.

For example, a property *investor* might set these criteria through rental yield and work to a plan that says that they will not buy property that cannot be developed into something that will produce a yield greater than the mortgage interest rate. On the other hand, a property *trader* might have financial criteria that say that they will not take on a project unless the profit on sale would create at least a 30% margin after payment of wages for their time and effort. These are basic financial criteria that you can use to guide your decision making. Do not compromise and use up your precious buying power for 'skinny' deals — mediocre acquisitions that aren't aligned with your ultimate strategy of achieving wealth through investment.

Set rules and stick to them. Your rules are there to protect you from you!

Pay attention to detail

I am going to ask you to indulge me as a chartered accountant and let me take you through a topic some people consider boring — but it's vitally important — that of record keeping and attention to detail. It is unfortunate that bookkeeping work carries a stigma because, really, it is so fundamental to you achieving a good result with your wealth creation.

Another maxim from the accounting world is 'what you can measure, you can manage'. Bookkeeping is the building block of measurement. Without it, you have no chance of reviewing and assessing your investments and monitoring the success or otherwise of your strategies.

Basic record keeping is the process of tracking and recording all of the relevant financial data for your affairs. These days there is no excuse for bad record keeping as there are inexpensive and fabulously powerful accounting packages available, some customised to different industries and some even specifically aimed at property investors.

So what is good record keeping? It involves using a separate bank account where all relevant transactions are captured. When we say "all relevant transactions", we mean everything, even the little stuff.

Count the small stuff

Let me ask you a question: If you were walking down a street and saw a one dollar coin on the footpath, would you bend over and pick it up? If you answered 'yes' to this question, you should create a system that tracks and records a three dollar expense/receipt because the one dollar coin and the three dollar tax receipt are worth the same amount of money. If, say, you pulled three dollars out of your pocket to buy an item for your property investment business — screws, glue, stationery etc — and you failed to record it in your accounting system, you lost one-third of that expense (because the tax deductibility would have been worth a third of the cost).

While you might think, "It's only a dollar", all of those dollars add up. The overall outcome that investors who have really good quality record keeping achieve is always far in excess of those who put little time and effort into tracking and recording their expenses properly.

Reconcile your bank accounts

In my accountancy firm we see many people who have attempted to diligently schedule the expenses that they flow through their business bank accounts, but then fail to prove that they have correctly captured this data by not reconciling the bank account. Bank reconciliation is a belts-and-braces approach to your bookkeeping that proves not only to yourself but also to your accountant (and to the IRD) that the data you have recorded in your spreadsheets, accounting systems or even cash books has been correctly entered without mistake and without omission.

The process of reconciling a bank account simply involves taking the opening balance of the account, adding all the funds that have entered the account, subtracting all the funds that have left the account and showing that the resulting balance agrees with the bank statement after adjusting for unpresented cheques and deposits.

I've lost track of the number of times clients have presented their end of year papers to our office and said, "Yes, Mark, it's all correct. Everything's there." But when we sit down and add up all the inwards and subtract all the outwards, we don't come within a bull's roar of the balances on the bank statements. This creates a real dilemma for an accountant because all we know for sure is that the financial outcome is not correct, but the process of actually identifying the errors is massively time consuming and expensive. It's far better if the clients put that little bit extra effort into reconciling their accounts on a regular basis — perhaps on receipt of each bank statement or, if required, even on a weekly basis — so that the task of finding any errors that occur is made easier.

A little tip: if you find that your bank reconciliation does not balance, one of the common mistakes is that you have transposed a figure. For example, 98 might have been written down as 89. If the amount that you are out by is divisible by 9, it is likely that the error is the transposition of a figure because the difference between 89 and 98 will always be divisible by 9. This is true for all transposed figures and can give you a clue as to the problem that you are trying to solve.

Monitor your investments

Prospering has got a lot to do with knowing where you stand and setting appropriate financial goals. In my view, the accumulation of properties for the sake of properties fits into the category of an inappropriate financial goal. A far more useful financial goal is the production of *profit* or *income* from the assets that you acquire.

When I studied accountancy we weren't taught very much about property, but we were taught how to analyse the *return on investment* — this is something I believe too few property investors spend enough time thinking about. But making your money work hard is crucial to your success.

If we agree that the goal for your investment is to ultimately produce a passive income (i.e. income that you do not have to work for) it is incredibly important that you monitor the returns that you are achieving from your assets, and make alterations to your plan and your portfolio if it's failing to meet the criteria that you have set for return. The irony for many property investors is that if the value of their assets is growing faster than the rental incomes, the returns that they are achieving are in fact *falling*.

This can be a little difficult to grasp because we often perceive our 'best' property to be the one which has given the most capital growth. But if that asset's *income* is not growing at the same pace, you're actually not moving towards your goal of achieving a passive income in retirement. You're simply becoming what I politely refer to as another of the world's poorest millionaires. There are many, many property investors in this category. They have significant wealth tied up in their assets but very poor cash flows and, unfortunately, low incomes.

The same can be said of many farmers, particularly sheep and cattle farmers, who at times live what amounts to a subsistence lifestyle on earnings from the farm, but retire (or die) rich as a result of the capital value of their assets. One farmer I know sold his farm and bought a string of commercial buildings in the town close to where he'd been farming. He'd basically swapped the farm for the commercial buildings. He told me a year later that the rents that he was receiving from the commercial buildings were producing an income for him for the first time in his life — and he had exactly the same amount of money invested in the properties as he'd had in the farm! He'd simply realised that his goal was to produce an *income*. The asset he had — the farm — wasn't achieving this, so he made a bold decision to exchange that particular asset for a different type of asset to produce the income that he was after.

This brings us to the concept of *opportunity cost*. If you understand how to calculate opportunity cost, you will find it much easier to analyse the returns on your assets. Here's a very simple example.

Say you have a property worth a million dollars that is producing 5% yield, i.e. $50,000 a year. Also in your portfolio of assets you also have a million dollars of debt. Interest rates have increased to 9%, so that debt is costing $90,000 per year to service interest-only. This means that your opportunity cost of retaining the million dollar property asset that is producing a 5% or $50,000 year return, is the *difference* between the rent received and the interest that would be saved if you sold that property and put the money into reducing other debt in the portfolio. Putting it another way, if the million dollar property was sold and the proceeds put into debt reduction, you would make a $90,000 per year interest saving. The opportunity cost of keeping the property earning $50,000 and the debt costing $90,000 is $40,000.

Now you might react to this by saying, 'Sure, but if I sell the property, I miss out on the capital growth.' This may well be true but the *certain* outcome is that if the property was sold and the debt reduced, your cash flow, your profit and your income would rise by $40,000 per year. It's then perhaps possible to take this reality and express it as a percentage of the value of the property.

Ask yourself, 'Do I believe the capital growth of the asset will be greater than the cash flow saved if the asset is sold and the debt repaid?' If you draw the conclusion that likely capital growth on the asset will not exceed the opportunity costs associated with keeping it, then in my view, the asset should simply be sold.

When I express this to people, many of them react with, "But Mark, if I do that I am just going to pay more tax!" This is true, but I feel that reaction falls into the category of not seeing the wood for the trees. Always remember, tax is just a by-product of income earned. It is ultimately better to have an income that is taxed than to have no income at all!

Financial decisions should always be made ahead of tax considerations because if a decision that would have increased income is not taken simply because there is more tax payable, then you've really missed an opportunity to prosper.

Unbundle your finance

Unbundling refers to a situation where property portfolios have developed over time with a limited number of lenders. As a result of this arrangement, in many cases assets will be cross-collateralised. This is not ideal at any time but especially not in a time of increased financial stress such as a weak property market.

If this is the case with you, work a strategy into your portfolio as you develop it to try to get a mix and separation of lenders. This is relatively easy to achieve when assets have appreciated to the point where deposits can be extracted from existing lending facilities to enable other lenders to take registered first mortgages over new acquisitions.

If one lender holds all your assets and you suffer adversity, the reality is that the lender will choose to sell whichever asset enables them to reduce the debt quickest — and that might not suit you. It's almost never likely to be aligned to your long-term wealth creation strategy.

Bringing these strategies to life

I would like to share a real example with you that involved clients of mine who made some significant changes to their lives. This shows how important it can be to understand the concept of opportunity cost.

This particular couple were hard-working kiwis who, early in their working lives, had acquired two beach properties side-by-side in a small town in New Zealand. Their plan was to reside in one property and rent the other to produce an income in retirement.

They had worked hard all their lives to repay the debts associated with the properties and had reached the point where the properties were debt free. In their early sixties they were still both working, but this was starting to take a toll on their personal health and well being.

They came to ask me for advice. The first thing we did was gather the facts around the properties. This simply involved getting both properties valued and looking at whether or not the property was fairly rented. A fairly common mistake that people make when assessing their opportunity costs is to do it based on the rental incomes that they are currently receiving — but if these rents are behind the market, sometimes quite wrong conclusions can be drawn.

So having determined the market rents and the values, we identified that the rental property had a valuation of approximately $900,000. But as it was only producing $350 a week this related to a 2% yield! Sure, because it was debt-free this was creating a passive income for the couple, but it was certainly not achieving their goal of allowing them to work less at a personal level … and it was certainly not an adequate return on the amount of money tied up in the property.

We discussed the idea of selling that rental property and reinvesting the money in a commercial property that would give, say, a 9% yield. This would see their incomes increase to about $81,000 per year — enabling them to stop work.

It took some time to convince them of the merits of this proposal. The beach property had increased significantly in value over the time that they had held it. They perceived it as being the one thing that had delivered them wealth. I agreed with them about that, but helped them see that at the point they were in their lives, the wealth was not providing them with the lifestyle that they had worked hard for and earned.

I also emphasised the point that by selling one property and buying another, the asset was being simply swapped around within the same asset class, i.e. still property, but as a commercial property investment their expectation of income could be met along with the continued expectation that the asset would continue to grow in value. I accepted that the commercial property asset may not necessarily grow in value at the same pace as the beach property — but none the less it was a good overall compromise.

My clients went away to think about this advice and ultimately decided to follow it. The process involved selling the investment property and taking professional advice to identify and acquire a well-let and managed commercial property investment. They did this, and the property immediately provided an income that enabled them both to retire on an income greater than they were earning from their personal work and effort.

Over the years since, they have used professional property managers to assist them to review the rents and progressively increase the income from the commercial building. As a result, the commercial building itself has continued to grow in value.

This simple example illustrates the principles of buying and holding property — but also of monitoring and reacting to falling yields as rental incomes and values of properties change. It also shows the value of being flexible enough to review these issues and react accordingly. These are very important aspects of not only creating wealth but also of making it work for you.

Mark Withers is the author of *Property Tax – A New Zealand Investor's Guide*. See recommended reading.

14

Navigating the legal issues when times get tough

Tony Steindle

As a lawyer I've experienced two downturns in the New Zealand economy. The first was when I first started work — a month after the 1987 sharemarket crash. The second was the 1998 Asian economic crisis. During the first downturn as a new fresh lawyer a common joke that circulated was: "What's the definition of optimism? Answer: A law graduate ironing five shirts on Sunday for the following week."

During these two downturns I saw some clients lose everything (including the shirt off their backs). I saw many others who spotted and took an opportunity.

What makes the difference is (1) being aware that the rules change during a downturn, and (2) operating with caution during this period.

Buying and selling residential property

In a lawyer's office, by far the most common indicators of a downturn are changing terms on Sale & Purchase agreements. As the cycle swings down you'll see more and more contracts that are conditional on the buyer selling an existing property. In good economic times buyers are tempted to make a purchase unconditional in the hope that they'd be able to raise bridging finance if needed. Bridging finance enables a buyer to dispose of another property in an orderly way. The problem with bridging finance is its cost (which can cripple an unprepared investor). Also, when the economy weakens you can't assume that you will always get finance — as banks, just like investors, get nervous.

In the late 1990s a client of mine fell in love with a lifestyle block. Against all advice (including the client's own family and me, the lawyer!) he went unconditional on the purchase. Settlement was to occur in six months. The client felt that there would be no problem selling his home and another investment property to fund the purchase. With the economy booming, he felt confident bridging finance would always be an option.

The dramatic 1998 Asian economic crisis occurred suddenly and with little warning. Most observers didn't understand the severity of its immediate and flow-on effects in its first few weeks. The financial collapse in Thailand, Malaysia, Indonesia and South Korea gave rise to massive currency devaluation, job losses and business collapses, not only in those countries which were most affected, but across the region. In New Zealand, as throughout the world, many investors and businesses with links to Asia found themselves under extreme financial pressure. Then forced property sales further depressed the local market as the crunch hit.

At the time I was on holiday in Asia *delighting* that my US dollars were getting more valuable by the day as local currencies plunged. Unfortunately for my client, the timing could not have been worse. His business struck tough times and, faced with the unfolding effects of the Asian crisis and restricting economy, banks (as they always do) started taking a more cautious view of lending. He made the best of a bad situation by dropping his asking price 10% on one property simply so he could settle his purchase. He managed to hold on to the second property long enough to get a more reasonable sale price. Ultimately, the exercise cost him over $50,000 (a lot more in today's terms).

So what could my client have done differently? For a start, he could have made the purchase conditional on him selling one or both of his existing properties. Alternatively, he could have made settlement much sooner. Agreeing to purchase a property at a future date means that you can benefit from an increase in value but, as in this case, it also means you can suffer the consequence of a value decrease as the market moves into a new cycle.

Selling

When selling a property in a softer market you may find you have a limited market or pool of potential purchasers — *much* more limited than you would have in a boom. Selling property during a downturn may also mean that to get your best price, you have to accept an offer conditional on the buyer selling another property.

In this case, it's vital that you as the seller insert a 'cash out' clause in the contract. A cash out clause means that during the conditional period of the contract (in this case conditional on sale of the purchaser's other property) if the seller receives a more favourable offer, the seller can cancel the first buyer's contract to buy. The only way that the first buyer can avoid cancellation of the contract is to make the purchase unconditional. Often this clause will allow the first buyer between three and five working days to make the contract unconditional. For you as the seller, this avoids the risk of losing a different cashed-up unconditional buyer by having to wait weeks for the first buyer to sell their property (which they may not sell, meaning your agreement with the first buyer fails). Some cash out clauses require that the second offer is unconditional; some just require the seller to be satisfied that the new offer is 'more favourable'. As a seller, try to use the looser version of the cash out clause — those which refer to 'more favourable' offers.

The seller's biggest risk in a falling market is a long term agreement to purchase. The reason for this is that although a purchaser may have had finance approved when they signed the agreement, this approval may not be issued at settlement.

In 1997 I had a client who contracted to buy an apartment. By the settlement date (sometime in 1999), the value of the apartment had fallen significantly below the agreed purchase price. (Yes, it happens!) In this case, the decrease was another result of the 1998 Asian economic crisis and its effect on property values). Not only did the fall in value cause a problem (with the loan-to-value ratio), but by 1999 banks had also changed their criteria for funding apartments — lending a significantly lower proportion of value than they had in 1997. My client could only proceed with the purchase after seeking funding from a second-tier lender — with subsequent higher interest rate and a broker's fee. (They were more lucky than some of the other buyers in that same development who lost their deposits.)

Among the most vulnerable property investors in a falling market are those tied into one or more contracts with terms like: "Pay just $1,000 today, settle in two years, and enjoy the capital gains between now and settlement". Oh yes. Remember: forecast capital *gains* can turn out to be capital *losses*.

Negotiating agreements in a falling market — some strategies

As a buyer, you are in a considerably better position to negotiate the price and deal you want when the property market is filled with doom and gloom.

During a boom most of the contracts we see in our law firm for residential property are either unconditional, or allow just a week for all conditions to be satisfied. In a boom, buyers also tend to take more risk than they otherwise would. For example, if a LIM report (Land Information Memorandum, a property report, obtained from a local authority) is not available in a week, some buyers will sign up *without* making the agreement conditional on seeing the LIM, through fear of losing the contract. This is definitely *not* a good idea, as I've seen many nasty surprises on LIM reports.

In contrast, when the slowdown occurs, buyers can much more readily dictate the terms of the offer which might include:

- The buyer having the time to make all their usual pre-purchase enquiries such as obtaining a building report, a LIM, and getting finance approval.

- Long term settlement.

- Right of access to the property before settlement.

- Vendor finance.

Time-bound offers

A useful strategy adopted by many property buyers is to make their offer only available for acceptance until a certain date and time. A common clause would say:

> "This offer is only open for acceptance by the Vendor until 4 pm on 12 July 2008, and if not accepted by the Vendor (time being strictly of the essence) by notice in writing by the Vendor to the Purchaser, this offer shall lapse".

The purpose of this clause is to put the heat on the seller to accept an offer, or risk losing it. In a strong market, this clause is hardly ever seen — sellers often have a multitude of possible buyers to negotiate with. But in a flat or falling market the boot is on the other foot and buyers are scarce. In these circumstances, this clause can be a useful strategy to obtain the type of agreement — and price — you want.

Auctions and tenders are also much less of a feature in a quiet market. Sellers won't want to risk holding an auction with no bidders because of the resulting stigma which attaches to the property. The one exception to this is mortgagee sales which are almost always conducted by auction and in the right circumstances can be a source of real bargains. I refer to the pitfalls of buying property at mortgagee sale in my book *Property Law – A New Zealand Investor's Guide* (see recommended reading). As a buyer, the risks are like any auction. If you are the successful bidder you'll usually need to pay 10% deposit at auction. You'll also need to ensure that the property is vacant on settlement. All the usual enquiries need to be made *before* bidding — such as a builder's report, LIM, and checking the title.

Buyers and sellers in trouble

Another situation that becomes more common when the property market and the economy slows is where the seller of a property cannot settle because their creditors won't allow the sale to go through. Usually this is because the proceeds from the sale aren't enough to cover associated debts.

The situation of a client of mine illustrates this scenario. That client was buying a substantial lifestyle block in Canterbury. The title to the property showed three mortgages, and caveats (which stop registration of the transfer of the land) to four others. The settlement date passed without the seller being able to give clear title. My client was within his rights to cancel the sale but didn't want to do so since he was sure he'd got a bargain. (He was correct; he got a bargain because the seller was in severe financial difficulty and under real pressure to sell — and sooner rather than later.)

The second reason my client didn't want to cancel the contract is that he'd paid a $100,000 deposit! This deposit went to the agent, who had already deducted their commission, *and paid the balance of the deposit to the seller.* Had my client cancelled the contract, he would have then been faced with suing the seller to retrieve his deposit — and my client could see that in that case he would just have joined a long queue of creditors, and probably incurred significant legal costs. (Not a *completely* bad thing from where I sit.)

The seller's mortgagees and caveat-holders couldn't agree how the sale proceeds would be applied (i.e. who among them would not be paid all that was owing). So my client was the victim of the seller's financial problems. In the end, thankfully, settlement did take place — but if it hadn't, my client would have been forced to negotiate with the holders of the mortgages to buy at mortgagee sale which could have meant him losing the property to a higher bidder — and he could have also lost the benefit of his $100,000 deposit.

The moral of this story is that even bargains attract risk. Had my client known more about the seller's financial plight (he didn't as he wasn't living in Canterbury at the time) we could have ensured that the deposit was tied up in a solicitor's trust account and not passed on to the agent or vendor until settlement.

As a seller of a property you also need to be wary of a buyer who can't meet their obligation to settle on time. The standard Sale & Purchase agreement includes a default rate of interest to be applied to late settlement, it gives sellers the ability to cancel the contract, and it details remedies you as a seller can pursue through the Court process. If the buyer simply cannot settle this can, on some occasions, be a disaster for the seller, particularly when the seller is relying on the proceeds from the sale to complete another purchase. One way to reduce this risk is to require a substantial deposit or to make sure bridging finance is readily available. The worst-case scenario is a cascade effect: to have a buyer default on you, and then lose the deposit you paid on a property you are contracted to purchase at the same time. My advice is to ensure that you get a sufficiently large deposit — to show that the buyer is substantial and to expose them to risk of loss if the deal falls over. ('Hurt money' it's sometimes called.) Even when you are finding it difficult to sell a property, you should demand a large deposit.

Vendor finance

Vendor finance also becomes more common when there is a shortage of buyers in the market. It can be a good way for buyers to fund a purchase when lenders at the same time are nervous about the state of the economy and tighten up.

A good example of this as a successful strategy was a deal involving clients of mine who wished to buy two sections of land. The sections were side by side on the Auckland city fringe — in what was then a run-down area. The original buildings had been demolished in the late 1980s to make way for a building project which failed to get off the ground. By 1991 the owner was desperate to sell, and agreed to a price of $120,000 per section. My clients were able to borrow two-thirds of the purchase price from a solicitors nominee company, raising $80,000 per section, and the seller was willing to leave in $30,000 per section as vendor finance.

My clients had to find only $10,000 each to buy.

They repaid the vendor finance in 1994, when the economy was a little stronger, using increased borrowings made possible by the rise in property values. (No extra 'cash' was needed, just servicing ability for the extra loan repayments.) In 2005 both sections were sold for $1.6 million. Through this deal my clients had been able to amass a very valuable asset — by just using $10,000 per section.

The common terms of vendor finance, when it was last popular, were for a fixed two-year term second mortgage with an interest rate usually between 2% and 5% above the current bank mortgage rate.

There is risk for the seller in offering vendor finance. If you're considering offering it to assist a sale, don't treat this as a do-it-yourself exercise. Usually your lawyer will prepare a document known as a *deed of priority* to establish how the proceeds of any sale of the property will be shared between the first and second mortgage holders during the term of the vendor finance. Interest on the first mortgage will take precedence over the second mortgage — which can erode the security of the vendor. As a seller be careful to obtain and use the correct paperwork. You must, for instance, be sure to obtain a *properly documented* loan agreement and personal guarantees from your buyer(s).

Protecting your assets — a balancing act

Family Trusts are used for a variety of purposes including creditor protection, saving tax, protecting an inheritance and avoiding claims by spouses and de facto partners. What I've noticed is that during a property boom, people tend to focus on saving tax — and sometimes this can be at the expense of creditor protection. You need to balance the sometimes conflicting outcomes.

One of my clients, for instance, is a very successful property developer. He has accumulated over $2 million in equity over the last five years. Recently a tax structure has become available to him which would enable him to significantly reduce his tax obligations. Broadly, this arrangement would allow him to transfer profits from several trusts to a business associate who has accrued tax losses but doesn't have the income to 'use' those tax losses. My client would get a tax benefit of $100,000 in the current financial year. The business associate would also receive a tax benefit so it would be beneficial for both parties. The structure is complex, but the end result would be that all of his equity would end up in his own name. (Without the tax planning structures this equity would have been held by trusts.)

As a developer my client routinely gives unlimited personal guarantees which exceed $20 million. The dilemma he faced was, which of these two to make the priority:

- Saving $100,000 in tax, or

- Protecting $2 million in assets.

After thinking about it long and hard, and taking into account that he has two young children, his decision was to forgo the tax benefits and protect the assets. The risk is too great compared to the benefit.

Risk control: timeliness of set up and asset transfers

This same client of mine had set up his legal structures some five years ago to protect his home, his holiday home, and personal assets from creditors. Take note: If you are going to engage in business or investment activities with risks associated (and realistically, that includes almost any activity), it is vitally important that these structures are set up correctly years before the risk occurs.

The Insolvency Act 2006 has specific provisions to set aside the transfer of assets to a trust where such transfers are intended to defeat the interests of existing creditors — or transfers which have occurred so close to the date of insolvency that it can be assumed that this was the purpose. If there are creditor risks, and *before* possible financial hardship is on the horizon, now is the time to set up a trust. Disposing of assets to a trust when you are in difficulty will, if challenged, almost certainly be set aside.

Bankruptcy

Many of our most successful property developers and investors today have been bankrupt, some more than once. How they were able to recover was often a factor of their determination, but for some, assets held in trust have enabled them to start again.

The Insolvency Act deals with bankruptcy. If a judgment is entered against you, and you cannot pay, the creditor can apply to the High Court to bankrupt you.

When you become bankrupt you cannot be in business or trade for three years. Although the period of bankruptcy is three years, credit reporting agencies will be aware of the bankruptcy for many years to come, and in practical terms five years passes from the bankruptcy until a bank will consider that the 'slate' is clean. Also, any surplus income earned during the period of bankruptcy must be paid to the Official Assignee (this is the government body that collects funds from the bankrupt person, can sell their property, and distributes funds to creditors). For all of these reasons bankruptcy is best avoided!

A simple way to avoid being vulnerable yourself is to *avoid giving a personal guarantee.* This is not as simple as it seems. When borrowing to buy property, personal guarantees are normally one of the bank's essential requirements. For business transactions there is more room to negotiate, and it's usually relatively easy to avoid giving personal guarantees to trade suppliers.

The importance of gifting

With trusts you also need to take into account that an individual can only gift to a trust $27,000 each year. Therefore it can take some time to complete a gifting programme. Until that's complete, the trust *owes a debt to you* for the assets transferred — and this debt is an asset in itself that your creditors can pursue. The sooner you start gifting, the sooner this transferral will finish, relieving you of the 'asset' of the trust's debt. (Another reason to transfer early is that any capital gain on an asset in a trust will accrue to the trust. It doesn't need to be gifted.)

Let me emphasise that if you are taking business or investment risks, especially for a developer or trader in property, it is important to set up a trust *sooner rather than later* and protect lifestyle assets such as a home and holiday home by transferring those assets to the trust and starting a gifting programme to reduce your personal assets.

Aside from the use of trusts to protect assets, there are other ways to reduce risk. Being beholden to just one lender is a risk. If rents decline, business profits diminish, and capital values decrease, banks and lenders can (and do) become involved and this can get messy. A good way to reduce this risk is to use more than one lender. In particular, use a separate lender to fund your home and lifestyle assets. Borrow elsewhere for your investment property. If you need to have a mortgage over your home (which should be owned in a trust, hopefully), try to keep that mortgage low compared to your investment properties; this lowers your personal risk.

Even if your trust still owes you a substantial amount of money there are ways to reduce risk. Back in 1995 a husband and wife I acted for owned a substantial home, and the husband ran a business in the building industry. To lower risk they agreed to enter into a contracting out agreement under the Matrimonial Property Act (now the Property Relationships Act). The effect of this agreement was that the husband would have full control of the business and two sections of land, and the wife would own the family home. The wife then transferred the home into a family trust and she started a gifting programme to that trust.

Just three years later the building downturn sparked by the Asian economic crisis caused severe financial difficulties for the building company. By 1999 a receiver was appointed and all of the building company's assets were lost. The husband's personal guarantees were called up and his creditors demanded funds from the family trust owning the home, and another trust which owned the two sections.

After protracted arguments the creditors had to agree that they had no claim on the home as it was clearly owned by the wife's trust. So they then sought to claim the debt owed by the husband's trust to him. The document acknowledging that debt showed it had been partly gifted and the balance owed by the trust to the husband was only to be paid after 25 years. This *properly executed and recorded paperwork* enabled the husband to negotiate a lower payment to settle with the creditors. He sold one of the sections to pay this debt. The result of this structuring was that, faced with a serious business failure, the family were able to keep their home (which was the roof over their children's heads) as well as a section and some assets to start again.

If the husband and wife in this example had delayed implementing this structure until, say 1997, the assets would have been lost. This example illustrates the need for forward planning, and thinking about what assets should be kept separate. Importantly, they also withstood the temptation to give a lender a mortgage over the home to support the business when they were encouraged to do this. If they had agreed to do so, they would have lost their home.

A warning: this type of structure should not be entered into lightly. If the couple had separated in the significant stress of those days, the husband would have had next-to-nothing in assets. Thankfully, and despite all of the financial pressure, they remain happily married.

Sham trusts

Even those with existing trusts need to be aware of the risk of their trust being declared a 'sham trust' by a court. Sometimes this follows application by the IRD or a creditor seeking to defeat the asset protection the trust offers. A trust is considered to be a sham if it cannot be shown to operate as a truly *independent* trust. Features of trust management which could see it classed a sham include:

- Where trust funds are intermingled with personal funds.

- Where there is inadequate record-keeping of decisions made by trustees.

- Where the trust either does not have an independent trustee, or if it has one, this trustee is not properly consulted.

It can be useful to get your lawyer to carry out a 'warrant of fitness' check for the trust to ensure it does indeed offer the creditor protection it was set up to provide.

Check your loans

In preparation for a downturn, check the finance terms of your existing loans. Many interest-only loans have fixed terms. For example, an interest-only loan may require the entire principal to be repaid in two years. You may have an expectation, based on past experience, that you'll simply 'roll over' the interest-only period at the same time as the loan — but in tougher times it might not be quite so automatic.

Lenders use this short-term arrangement to ensure that if the market drops they are not exposed to an interest-only loan where the principal owed may end up being more than the asset itself. (It happens.) For this reason, even where repayments can end up being higher, switching your loan to say, a 25-year principal-and-interest loan, *before* any difficulties arise may avoid a nervous lender calling up its securities.

Needing to sell when circumstances change

There are a number of reasons why property is sold, aside from it being an investment decision. These include:

- A downturn in the business of the investor, or losing their job as an employee when redundancy occurs.

- A relationship ending and property being sold to pay out a partner or spouse.

- Moving overseas or to a different town or city.

- The investor suffering illness, disability or death.

Although it initially seems that there is nothing that can be done about these issues I have had clients who have faced personal crises who have not lost money on the property market. These have included:

- A self-employed client who entered into an arrangement with creditors to buy time. In this case the client gave security over several properties to enable him to keep those properties and ride out the storm.

- A business where the outlook was not good. In this case rather than face a loss of all of that client's investment properties, and then the business failing, a pragmatic decision was made to cease trading in the business and not risk the loss of personal assets.

- A family deciding to fund the mortgage of their deceased mother to maximize the sale price and waiting over a year to sell the deceased mother's home, and renting it out in the meantime.

- A couple who separated unable to agree on anything, but while still documenting the separation agreement, kept the beach property for almost two years after they separated until the market improved.

Commercial leasing

When economic conditions are tight it is possible for landlords to lose what were once strong tenants. (After all, prior to the 1987 crash shares in, for example, Equiticorp were considered blue chip stock, and that company, among others which later failed, was considered a blue chip tenant. Times change.)

In a downturn, when a vacancy arises, prospective tenants have much more leverage to negotiate the tenancy they want.

Common clauses asked for by commercial tenants from landlords in these tighter economic times include:

- **Rent holidays** – A rent holiday is where the landlord gives the tenant rent-free use of the premises (for say, three months) as an incentive to sign up for a lease. If you're giving a tenant a rent holiday it can still be valuable to get two months' rental deposit — in the worst-case scenario, the tenant takes the three months free rent and then disappears. A rental deposit at the very least shows that a tenant has the means to pay the rent when the holiday comes to an end. (Normally the tenant's share of outgoings remain payable during the rent holiday.)

- **Cap on outgoings** – Another inducement offered by keen commercial landlords is restricting the amount of outgoings (property expenses like rates, insurance) payable by the tenant. If you agree to this, make sure you *limit the term* of this discount to say, the first two years of the lease. When times get better you wouldn't want to be bound by this restriction for years to come. Landlords who make this mistake regret it because they've reduced their income (and hence, value) for the life of that lease.

- **Decreased lease term** – A tenant will often seek a short term lease (say two years) and then ask for a number of rights of renewal, say two years each. Agreeing to this arrangement gives your tenants effective control over your premises for the length of the rights of renewal. It also gives them leverage whenever you seek a rent review. They will often say: "I'll renew the lease, but only if you leave the rent the same." If agreeing to this stipulation is unavoidable, at least *limit the period to which it applies.*

It is much better, for example, to agree to a two-year lease with one right of renewal for two years, than to sign up to give the tenant five two-year rights of renewal. The former option means that, after the first four years, you can negotiate a more landlord-friendly lease when the economy has (hopefully) improved.

- **Fitout contribution** – In a market where tenants are scarce you may also be asked for a cash contribution towards your prospective tenant's fitout. Think this over carefully. A fitout contribution, combined with a rent holiday could be very costly to a landlord. If you agree to a fitout contribution (and only do so if it's absolutely necessary to get the tenant you want) make sure at the very least that it's capped to a *specific agreed amount* and only to be paid when the work is completed. Whether or not you agree to make a contribution should also depend in part on how valuable the work would be for future tenants. For example, a client of mine contributed towards tenant fitout of offices where the layout was not suitable for other similar tenants. Later it had to be *removed at the landlord's cost* (ugh) when the tenant company went into receivership. Also, be careful to make it clear who owns the fitout. If the fitout is owned by the tenant, under the standard lease the tenant has the option to remove it (so long as they restore the premises to the same condition they were in before the fitout was installed). If they do not remove it, the landlord can require the tenant to pay the costs of restoration. If the fitout is owned by the landlord, the landlord has to meet restoration costs but this can be useful to future tenants as the existing tenant has no right to remove it. There is a significant difference between these two scenarios and the choice made as to ownership of the fitout depends on its value.

- **Personal guarantees** – Even if you are desperate for a tenant, do not fail to get a personal guarantee from your tenant or its directors. Personal guarantees are a factor in valuation and could significantly impact the price you would receive if selling (or funding) the property later. If pressed, you could negotiate limiting a personal guarantee to, say, one year's rental.

As a landlord, it is *always* worth investigating to check how financially reliable your commercial tenant actually is — likewise, their personal guarantors. A client of mine requires all prospective tenants to complete a statement of assets and liabilities, and sometimes requires a credit check. (You should have their written consent before you arrange a credit check.) This is even more important when the tenant wants favourable terms such as a fitout contribution or rent holiday. It is all very well attracting a new tenant to your property, but if you've waived rent (or actually *paid* for their renovations) an insolvent tenant can put you in a much worse position than you were with vacant premises.

It is also important to consider your mix of tenants in multiple unit properties — and the potential impact of a new tenant on other tenants. This is even more essential if your tenants have a ready choice of alternative premises. For example, a client of mine owned an industrial property where two of his five tenancies were empty. Under significant financial pressure from a downturn, he leased one of the vacant units to a firm of panel beaters — a good solvent business.

Unfortunately, the other tenants weren't happy with the noise and felt that the presence of the panel beater lowered the tone of the building and brought their businesses into disrepute. In a short space of time, two of the existing tenants had their leases' rights of renewal come up. They declined to renew their leases and left. The landlord now had *three* vacancies (instead of two) and it became harder to attract new tenants because of the panel beaters.

Relying on others

If I have ever seen dramatic loss occur quickly, it is when business partners or partners in a joint venture fail to perform their part of the deal.

There are many advantages to going into business with others. The principal reason given is to spread the risk, and spreading risk is useful when times are tough. The most common other reason for forming a partnership or joint venture is where each partner needs the other to achieve the deal. For example, one partner may have the income needed to service the purchase, while the other has the equity to make the purchase possible. In certain types of property investment, one partner may have a knowledge or skill needed by the other. Sometimes it works out, sometimes it doesn't.

An example of this (which nearly cost my clients the shirts off their backs) was a project to build a retirement village. My clients had skills in property development; their joint venture partner had rest home industry skills. The intention was to build and then run a rest home and hospital facility. Surrounding units would be built and sold to residents.

My clients were to deal with development, while the joint venture partner was to provide their expertise in this industry, run the rest home and hospital and, crucially, fund half of the equity needed for the project. Since the partners were on good terms, there was no written agreement. This is *always* a mistake.

My client agreed to buy the land and signed an unconditional contract. Unfortunately, around that time, his joint venture partner lost a significant amount of money on a completely unrelated project. By the time of settlement this partner had no funds to contribute. The joint venture then fell apart. My clients had no choice but to proceed. Over the following two years they had to sell all of their other assets. They also had a steep learning curve trying to figure out how to care for elderly patients and prepare breakfast, lunch and dinner for sixty residents.

They considered taking the joint venture partner to court, but the partner had no available assets. An action to recover their losses in court would have been fruitless and costly, and they had little choice but to proceed with the project themselves.

As the saying goes, hindsight is a wonderful thing, but how could this have been different?

Well, firstly, my clients could have (and should have) properly investigated the financial circumstances of their joint venture partner. They should have insisted on full disclosure of their financial position, and found out about the problems before committing to the unconditional purchase.

Secondly, a formal agreement between the parties would have made it easier and more cost-effective to recover their losses through the court. A proper joint venture agreement would have had a clause requiring penalty interest to be paid, making full legal costs payable on a default, and personal guarantees could have been provided for, in the case of a partner failing to fulfil their obligations. In this situation there would have been nothing to recover, but that's not always the case.

Fortunately, this was one sad story with a happy ending. Despite a few years of stress and worry, the retirement village was ultimately a success. They expanded it into a second stage a few years later, and the profits from the retirement village have set my clients up for life.

Get it in writing

Often the excitement of a purchase or project can see formally documenting an arrangement with others deferred. In my experience, the process of merely recording the arrangement (and the partners' understanding if it) in writing can deal with the many 'what ifs' associated with a joint transaction.

When you purchase property with another person or party, it's *essential* that you also have a clear path to sell or exit the property deal. One fairly tidy way is for two or more individuals to buy a property using a company where they each hold an equal number of shares.

A separate agreement will deal with selling the property. Without such an agreement there is no ability for one shareholder to require that the property be sold — meaning their equity could be locked up in a property, even if that equity is needed by one party for another purpose or transaction.

Such an agreement also needs a mechanism to deal with the situation where, for instance, one party fails to pay their share of the mortgage or other property expenses. It's common for this clause to give the other party the right to acquire the defaulting party's shareholding — at a price which takes into account the costs of the default — if they are left to carry the burden of that obligation.

Property development and trading

Developing and trading property are the areas of property law which attract the greatest risk. The reason for this is that the time period between purchasing, obtaining resource and building consents, constructing or renovating and then finally *selling* property can (and frequently does) take more than a year. This time delay often leaves developers particularly exposed and vulnerable to a change in market conditions.

As a developer of multi-unit property (e.g. a subdivision) it is important that you make any sales of property *conditional* on obtaining project funding and there being a sufficient number of sales to justify the project proceeding.

A client of mine recently purchased a motel block. His offer was conditional on a two-month due diligence period — during which time he sought a business operator for the motel. He was successful in doing this (although later in the project). At the same time, he offered the individual units for sale to investors on the basis that they would lease the units back to the motel operator.

Only *five* of the twenty-six units were sold by the time he went unconditional on the purchase. (Also, at the time of going unconditional he had not finally agreed terms with the business operator.) So going unconditional was, of course, a significant risk if there had been a downturn in the market. When he started the project in early 2007 the property market was still booming and he has since sold all the units to investors *and* the motel business. This same strategy might have considerably less chance of success in a flat or falling market.

My client mitigated his risk by making all of the contracts for sale to investors conditional on the project proceeding. The exit strategy available to him, therefore, was to cancel the sale contracts and sell the motel block as it was — perhaps with an operator in place. There would have been no profit (and likely even a loss), but at least he would have avoided the obligation to proceed with the development with too few purchasers. His view was that it would have been easier to sell the motel as a whole than to try to sell individual units if the market deteriorated. He was clear beforehand about his exit strategy.

It's still possible to do well as a property trader in a falling market. The biggest cost with trading is often the holding costs paid (the biggest of these being finance interest). This cost can be reduced by agreeing with the seller to a long term settlement and a right of access prior to settlement (which can also include a right to do work on the property). This enables a buyer to undertake the bulk of any work required before settlement occurs. Often a trader will successfully get the purchase to occur on the same date as their on-sale.

Last words

A downturn in the market creates both risk and opportunity. I'm occasionally asked how we lawyers cope with a slowed economy. My somewhat unedifying response to such inquirers is that while our property transaction work slows, we undertake much more work in trust formation, brush up on our knowledge of insolvency law, and get prepared for the influx of relationship property work when couples fall apart as a result of financial pressure. (This pretty much confirms the commonly held view that society has of lawyers — but unfortunately it's also true!)

The reality is that as a lawyer I see some very stressed and over-committed clients who suffer the consequences of a falling market, and others who profit over time from a market correction. Whether you as an investor suffer or profit depends on how prepared you are for the inevitable fall in the market, and how adaptable you are in changing how you 'do business' over this time.

Tony Steindle is the author of *Property Law – A New Zealand Investor's Guide*. See recommended reading.

Acknowledgements

Producing a book is a team effort; this one more so than most. I'd like to acknowledge the contributors to this project, my friends Tony Steindle, Mark Withers, Mike McCombie and Andrew King, for their enthusiasm and their commitment to creating something of value. The journey was longer than we anticipated, with a few challenges, but I feel we can be proud of what we have created together. Thank you.

Thanks to Olly Newland, Mark Munro and Rex Jensen for so willingly sharing their experience and their insights on property cycles, and to Tim Julian for his wry, recognisably true commercial property clock. Thanks to Westpac's Brendan O'Donovan, my kind of economist: a straight shooter not afraid to take a position, and to Dr Garrick Small whose research penetrates the pseudo-science.

I'd also like to acknowledge Dolf de Roos and Robert Kiyosaki. Time spent talking with these two teachers over the years has had a profound influence on my thinking.

Once again I'm enormously grateful to my friend and mentor Roger Steele, who is willing to press a point but always with good humour. Roger, your high standards and clarity are an inspiration.

Special thanks to Sarah Bolland and Shelley Dixon whose sharp eyes, language skills and sense of style helped the expression of ideas and the flow of the book.

Each of the authors and I recognise the key part our families have played in this project by their support in many ways (not least their tolerance of our distraction) during the book's gestation. We acknowledge them with grateful thanks.

— Peter Aranyi

Recommended reading

- *Beating the Property Clock* Ajay Ahuja

- *Commercial Real Estate Investor's Guide* Peter Aranyi

- *Conquer the Crash* Robert R Prechter Jr

- *Create Wealth: The Complete Guide to Residential Property Investment* Andrew King & Lisa Dudson

- *Long Term Property Prices: Implications for Sydney Residential Development* Garrick R Small (a paper presented to the International Cities Town Centres & Communities Society Conference Sydney 2008)

- *Lost Property* Olly Newland

- *Planning for Property Success* Andrew King

- *Property Hotspots Around the World* Ajay Ahuja

- *Property Law – A New Zealand Investor's Guide* Tony Steindle

- *Property Tax – A New Zealand Investor's Guide* Mark Withers

- *The Bubble of American Supremacy* George Soros

- *The Day the Bubble Bursts* Olly Newland

- *The Rascal's Guide to Real Estate* Olly Newland

- *The Significance of Debt, Human Nature and the Nature of Land on Real Estate Cycles* Garrick R Small and Jacob Oluwoye (a paper presented to the Pacific Rim Real Estate Society International Conference Sydney 2000)

- *The Winning Investment Habits of Warren Buffett & George Soros* Mark Tier

Recommended resources

Real Estate Master mortgage calculator for commercial or residential investors

Put answers to mortgage funding and interest payment questions at your fingertips. This powerful yet easy-to-use calculator has been designed for people in real estate who need to quickly and easily calculate amortisation and payments on principal-and-interest mortgages, or future values.

Unlike some financial calculators, the function keys are clearly labelled in English. You use buttons marked 'Term', 'Pmt' (payment) 'Int' (interest rate) and Loan Amt (loan amount). You can use any three of these to find the fourth, then change a variable and quickly recalculate the results.

You can easily calculate weekly, fortnightly, monthly or annual payments—in fact *any* number of payments per year. Or work backwards from payments, term and interest rate to a loan amount. It has lots of clever features to make using it *easier*.

If all this sounds complex, it's not. By quickly working through the examples in the instruction booklet you'll be confident in no time. It really is the simplest, most powerful calculator in its class. *Money-back satisfaction guarantee.*

For more details, and to order: www.EmpowerEducation.com
Phone +64 9 535 2415 or 0800 66 22 55

www.EmpowerEducation.com

Empower Education aims to offer the best independent financial education and training available and to bring you learning tools and resources that will empower you for success.

Programmes

- Real Estate, Sharemarket, & Business Success events

- 3 Hours to Freedom® Club

- Financially Free Families™

- The B.E.S.T® Business & Entrepreneurial Skills for Today

- Financial Academy for Youth®

- Personal development programmes

Educational resources and products

- Robert Kiyosaki's CASHFLOW® games, books, tapes, etc

- Books, tapes, and software on Wealth and Finances, Business Success, and Personal Development

For more information and news of upcoming
financial education events and resources, contact:
Empower Education Ltd
PO Box 39 115 Howick, Auckland 2145, New Zealand
Phone +64 9 535 2415   Fax +64 9 535 2416
info@EmpowerEducation.com

Making Money in Commercial Property™ Seminar

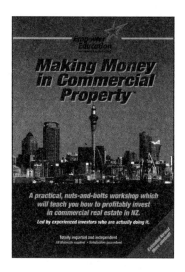

Your chance to learn in person from experienced commercial property investors.

While learning from a good book has its advantages, sometimes the best way to gain confidence and skills in an area is to get alongside experienced people, hear their stories and ask questions.

Empower Education offers a two-day seminar on commercial property investment. *Making Money in Commercial Property™* is a practical, nuts-and-bolts workshop which will teach you how to profitably invest in commercial real estate.

These informal weekend events are led by experienced investors who are actually doing it. The intensely practical course covers the nitty-gritty of commercial property. No fluff.

The speakers are active investors with decades of experience. They share their experiences and lessons learned, and teach you strategies for success using lots of real-world examples and case studies.

If you see commercial real estate in your future, then this lively, interactive course gives you the chance to benefit from the experience of a group of successful local commercial property investors.

> For details of the next course being offered,
> call Empower Education +64 9 535 2415 or 0800 66 22 55
> or email info@EmpowerEducation.com

Property Tax
–A New Zealand
Investor's Guide

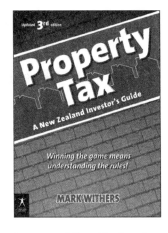

Winning the game means
understanding the rules

Mark Withers

A lively, easy-to-read book on a vital topic for every New Zealand property investor, this is a concise guide to essential information about tax—information you need to succeed in property. Accessible, written in plain English with lots of practical examples, this book covers the key issues of taxation affecting property investors in New Zealand.

Accountant and property investor Mark Withers explains areas that can seem complex, such as rental yields, financial structures, and what can and can't be claimed. He shares his strategies for success as an investor and provides valuable hints for avoiding trouble with the IRD, based on ten years' experience as an accountant and property investor.

Mark Withers is an Auckland chartered accountant specialising in tax advice for property investors. He is a popular speaker at property investors' conferences and a successful commercial and residential investor himself, a founding member of the Auckland Property Investors Association, and director of accountancy firm Withers Tsang & Co.

Empower Leaders Publishing Ltd.
ISBN 978-0-9582307-9-7
At good bookstores or on-line at **www.EmpowerEducation.com**

Also by Mark Withers:
The 7 Key Traits of Successful Property Investors audio programme
Available from Empower Education.

Property Law – A New Zealand Investor's Guide

Know the facts – avoid the traps!

Tony Steindle

An easy-to-follow guide to New Zealand real estate law. Written by an investor, for investors, *Property Law* demystifies and explains the key legal issues in property transactions — and shows you how to avoid the traps.

Contents include:

- Contracts and agreements – and disputes

- Your rights, obligations and protections when buying, selling, leasing, building, developing or subdividing

- What to watch out for on a title

- Buying off the plans

- Residential landlord and tenancy issues

- District Plans and the Resource Management Act

- Working with builders, construction contracts

- Commercial real estate — due diligence, understanding commercial leases and tenancies

Property Law uses practical examples and real cases to show how the law works – and how it affects you. With useful checklists and plain English definitions of legal terms, this book is essential for anyone investing in property.

Empower Leaders Publishing Ltd.
ISBN 978-0-9582746-1-6
At good bookstores or on-line at **www.EmpowerEducation.com**

Commercial Real Estate Investor's Guide

Making money as a commercial property investor in New Zealand

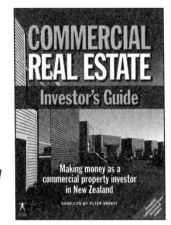

compiled by Peter Aranyi

This no-nonsense, comprehensive book covers the detail and nitty-gritty of successful commercial property investing. Presented in clear, accessible language, and loaded with lots of real-world examples, *Commercial Real Estate Investor's Guide* sheds light on the key issues surrounding investing in commercial and industrial property. Get the benefit of experience.

This book brings together vital information from a group of experienced local investors and experts who share their frank advice for making money as an investor.

Whether you're a novice or seasoned investor, this book will fill gaps in your knowledge and show you how to succeed in this field.

Based on years of research and combined experience, this independent and impartial handbook is *essential* reading for all investors in commercial and industrial property in New Zealand.

Empower Leaders Publishing Ltd.
ISBN 0-9582307-4-9
At good bookstores or on-line at www.EmpowerEducation.com

The Rascal's Guide® to Real Estate

A no-holds-barred handbook for investing in the real world.

Olly Newland lifts the lid on the teeming world of real estate — and shares secrets and tricks of the trade — in *The Rascal's Guide to Real Estate*.

With more than 40 years experience, Olly Newland spares no-one in his fourth book on real estate investment. He aims his flame-thrower at real estate agents, bankers, lawyers, financial planners, tenants of all sorts, property syndicate promoters — not to mention the many unscrupulous con artists he's come across during his career.

But *The Rascal's Guide to Real Estate* is much more than just a chance for an experienced investor to vent his spleen. Throughout more than 200 pages he dispenses valuable and intensely practical advice for those wanting to succeed as investors and landlords.

His subject matter ranges through dealing with agents, raising finance, negotiating deals, renovating houses or 'do-ups', advertising, selling on low deposit, investing in commercial and industrial property, auction tactics, and more — as well as dirty tricks to watch out for and how to safeguard yourself from hazards of the game. This book provides vital information to help today's investor get ahead.

Updated and expanded second edition.

Empower Leaders Publishing Ltd.
ISBN 0-9582746-0-6
At good bookstores or on-line at **www.EmpowerEducation.com**

Climbing the Property Ladder

How to Tales of Profit and (mis)Adventure in the Real Estate Jungle

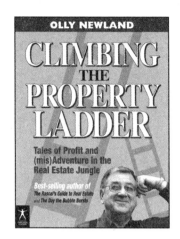

Veteran investor and best-selling author
Olly Newland shares lessons from 45 years as a property investor.
This book covers some of Olly's adventures as purchaser, landlord,
or vendor in property deals or (as is often the case) as a consultant
for others.

The stories have the common threads of real estate investment
and the common human failings of greed, fear, naivety, carelessness
and envy. Some have happy endings, some do not. Many are about
raw human emotion — property just happens to be involved along
the way.

In this book you will read about those who started with nothing
and made literally millions. Learn about the cheats, crooks and
downright criminals who are attracted to big money as moths to
a flame.

In his usual take-no-prisoners, entertaining style, Olly shares
valuable lessons and breathtaking stories about how property deals
can change people's lives.

Empower Leaders Publishing Ltd.
ISBN 0-9582307-7-3
At good bookstores or on-line at **www.EmpowerEducation.com**

Index

A

affordability 23, 41, 48, 76, 96
Asian economic crisis 163, 164, 166, 175

B

bankruptcy 92, 107, 108, 173
brokers – finance 40, 106, 150, 166
budding investors 30
Buffett. Warren 8, 11, 61, 64, 69, 72, 188
bullish new investors 35

C

calculator
    Real Estate Master IIx 189
capital growth 24
capitalisation rates 79
cash is king 136
cash flow 17, 25, 27-29, 32–37, 39–41, 46–49, 57, 72, 88, 89, 95–97, 105, 109, 110, 119, 125, 127, 129, 132, 145, 159
childcare industry 6
child support 149
Cinderella at the ball 11
clock depicting property cycle 72–75, 80
commercial property cycle 80–81
Commercial Real Estate Investor's Guide 9, 77, 140
confidence 78, 91
Conquer the Crash 68

cowboys 65, 103, 121, 123
Crash of 1987 65, 100, 102, 124, 128
credit check 106, 181
credit crunch 17, 64, 77
cycle of market emotions 8
cycles
    characteristics 74
    contraction phase 54, 59, 65
    in nature 53
    long term 66–69
    strategies for phases 24–29
    we prefer certain parts 53

D

debentures and GSAs 108
deed of priority 171
deposit 22, 31, 68, 105, 112–115, 168–170, 179
depression
    defined 63
    Great Depression 66
divorce 141–142, 146
dot-com boom 20

E

economic clock 72, 73
economists 4, 5, 11–13, 70
    professionals vs amateurs 11, 75–76
eldercare industry 6
Elliott Wave theory 66–68
emotion 9, 13, 20, 61, 91, 117, 196

F

G

H

I

J

K

L

M

N

O

P

R

recession
    defined 63
rent holiday 86, 130, 179
Reserve Bank 21, 70, 76, 124
respiratory cycle 52
risk 25, 71, 173

S

second-tier lenders 103
sham trust 176
sinking fund 105
Small, Garrick 75-77
social mood 9, 76
Soros, George 9, 61, 188
spruikers 11, 75
sub-prime 64, 68, 77
supply and demand 3, 6, 13, 19, 63
Sydney market 75–76

T

tenant demand 86
The Bubble of American Supremacy 9
The Day the Bubble Bursts 13, 188
The Hitch-hikers Guide to the Galaxy 18
The Winning Investment Habits of Warren
    Buffett and George Soros 61
time-bound offers 168
time lag 21
tithe and contribute 143
trend line 4, 5, 71, 82
Twain, Mark 57

U

unbiased information & commentary 2, 77
unintentional investors 30

V

vendor finance 61, 106, 111, 139, 171
vision 133–135

To obtain additional copies of this book

or any other Empower Leaders Publishing titles, please visit: **www.EmpowerEducation.com** Join the mailing list to stay up to date, and receive free impartial commentary and information.

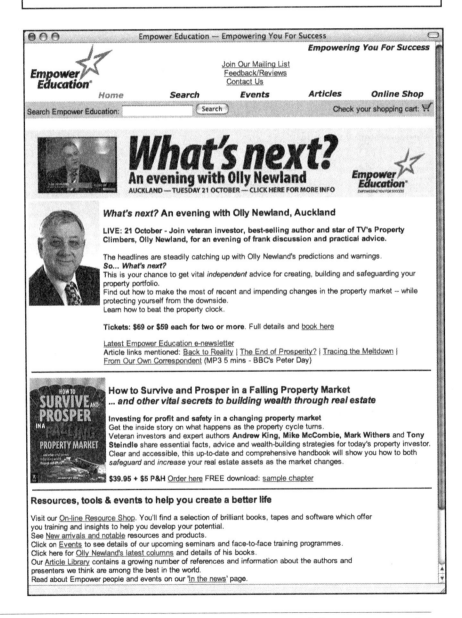

How to survive and prosper in a falling property market